MARY JO PENNINGTON

BIG ANGELS AND FLAMING WILD HORSES

FOREWORD BY
SHARNAEL WOLVERTON

Unless noted otherwise, all scriptures are taken from the New King James Version of the Bible.

The book **6 Big Big Big Angels** is referred to in this book as **6 Big Angels.**

Big Angels Ministries, Inc.
813-681-4993
www.6bigangels.com

International Standard Book Number: **0-9774489-2-4**

First Printing June 2007

Printed by
A & A Printers
Tampa, Florida

Original Cover Art By
Maylia G. Trahan
Baton Rouge, Louisiana

Published by
Big Angels Press
Valrico, Florida

restore hearts

MAYLIA G. TRAHAN
Prophetic Artist

"I Am – Courageous"

"When I called, you answered me; you made me bold and stouthearted" Psalm 138:3.

Horses are bold and stouthearted. Horses represent strength and courage. We too are made strong like horses displaying a posture of splendor. Like horses wearing a victor's wreath, we are a victorious people and will not stop short of complete victory.

"I Am – Courageous" represents uninhibited courage and spirit to run free. Do not allow the bridle to tame the desires God has put within us and hinder us from commanding the breakthrough that is ours through Christ Jesus.

A recurring vision for three years of three horses: One red, one black, and one white. The details become clearer with time and revelation. Conquering horses, red, white, and black thunder through the Apostle John's vision in the Book of Revelation chapter six.

In Zechariah chapter one, the angel of the LORD is riding a red horse accompanied by red, brown, and white horses patrolling the earth. The horses and their colors represent God's involvement in the governments of the world. The riders report to the angel of the LORD that the world is at peace.

"I Am – Courageous" represents breakthroughs of courage, freedom, strength and peace to each child of God personally, but God has expanded the revelation to encompass world governments in a vision of peace.

TABLE OF CONTENTS

INTRODUCTION

This book is a continuation of Victoria's heavenly experiences into the supernatural realm. There are some similarities to our first book "**6 Big, Big, Big Angels**." Some of the events described in the first book have been expanded with additional information that Victoria has provided since that book was written.

What we have written here are vivid accounts of a small child who was miraculously saved from severe injury or possible death. These are recorded events that clearly declare God's Glory manifested on earth.

Our commission now is to expand the knowledge of the Glory of God on earth. We are doing that by relating the reality of heaven as revealed to a small child.

Hab 3:3-4
3 His glory covered the heavens,
And the earth was full of His praise.
4 His brightness was like the light;
He had rays flashing from His hand,
And there His power was hidden.

Hab 2:3
3 For the vision is yet for an appointed time;
But at the end it will speak, and it will not lie.
Though it tarries, wait for it;
Because it will surely come,
It will not tarry.

Hab 2:14
14 For the earth will be filled With the knowledge of the glory of the LORD, As the waters cover the sea.

His Glory has always been here. It is the Knowledge of His Glory that is now being revealed.

> 1 Cor 2:9
> 9 But as it is written: "Eye has not seen, nor ear heard, Nor have entered into the heart of man the things which God has prepared for those who love Him."

Since the creation of man, God has hungered for close fellowship with His people. He has always yearned to walk with us and talk with us face to face.

The children of Israel have always been mighty and fierce warriors. Today's Israeli army is the bravest and most effective fighting force in the world. In the time of Moses, the presence of God was a fearsome thing even for these brave people. We can no longer be afraid of the supernatural. We must no longer say to Moses, "You go to talk to God. Then come back and tell us what He said."

God has been preparing the body to bear the heaviness and weight of His Glory. His Glory will grace every meeting when we come to worship Him. It is time to welcome His Glory.

We believe that the church is ready and hungry to hear about the wonders of heaven. It is past time for us to continue to drink milk. Now is the time to eat meat.

Many new born babies continue to drink milk for their first year with no solid food. However, at the age of five months, Victoria grabbed a bar-b-que rib from her Mommy's plate and started to gnaw on it. She has not stopped eating meat since that day.

If you are ready to enjoy the meat of God's Glory, read this book with an open spirit. Let Victoria tell you about "The Knowledge of The Glory of The Lord that is filling the earth as the waters cover the sea."

Dedications

This book is dedicated to Sandra Louise Nasworthy, our dear daughter and Mommy of Victoria Hanah-Rene Nasworthy.

Sandi has tirelessly recorded and documented the words of Victoria into the late hours of the night. Without her dedication this book would not have been possible.

During the time of my recuperation she stepped in and took over taking care of Grandpa and me with cooking and keeping up with the household tasks. This was done cheerfully even with the heavy load of her own life.

She has been a constant source of strength and stability to Grandpa and me. We have always relied on her faithful intercession to sustain us.

"Thank you" is nowhere near adequate to express my gratitude to her.

I love you, Sandi, "Mother of the Child."

Mom

Foreword

I cannot encourage you enough to read this book! You will be so transformed in your mind, body, soul and spirit as you turn each and every page of life giving revelation!

Mary Jo and Don Pennington, as well as Sandi and Victoria Nasworthy, are incredible models of life giving New Testament revolutionists! These guys are living the bible and sharing openly the availability of open heaven for everyone willing to receive!

This book will broaden your vision both in the natural and in the spirit. It will empower you to believe for yourself and your family for the supernatural realms like you have never imagined.

It will impart a gift of hunger and desperation in you that will allow you to stretch beyond the realms you currently walk in.

It will also impart faith and courage to any empty place within that held neither only moments before.

Walk through their journey and stumble to your own. I dare you!

Sharnael Wolverton
Swiftfire Ministries International
Denham Springs, Louisiana
www.swiftfire.org

A Word From Our Pastors

Don and Mary Jo Pennington are at the forefront of restoring to the church the awareness that we are created by God: Body, soul and *spirit*. To only be aware of what is going on through the five senses robs us of our inheritance as believers to worship God in spirit and in truth.

Throughout scripture we find those close to God and used by Him who discerned the environment of the spirit. Angels visited Abraham, Gideon, Samson's parents and Daniel. James, John and Peter saw and overheard a conversation Moses and Elijah had with Jesus. Peter had an angel awaken him in prison.

Dreams, visions, discerning of spirits, angels and visits to heaven are being reported more and more.

In the midst of these restored revelations, the Penningtons have found themselves drafted to serve in the forefront of the re-discovery of many biblical truths through the experiences of their granddaughter Victoria... as well as their own.

We have found Don and Majo to be releasers of joy to those they share with and imparters of faith to those whose faith has ebbed low.

We bless their testimonies in this second book chronicling their ongoing adventures with Father, Son and Holy Spirit.

Tom & Sue Breuner
Abundant Love Christian Fellowship
Washington, DC

Endorsements

JEFF JANSEN

Victoria is an incredible little girl with an equally incredible gift of seeing in the spirit.

I believe she is a forerunner of a new generation of Seers and wonderworkers that God is raising up to bring heaven to earth.

The heavenly encounters and visitations Victoria has with Jesus are not imaginary but are real and carry a powerful release. The impact of what Victoria and other young ones like her see and bring back for us is key to how God is moving now and will move in the future.

I fully endorse this ministry.

Jeff Jansen
Global Fire Ministries

A WORD FROM PASTOR THIERRY

Since reading my copy of 6 Big Angels, not only have I been blessed, but I've seen a growth among our Youth Department, simply because God used a child to send his message.

My church as a whole has experienced a greater awareness of the importance of Gods Power. The Bible said in Matthew, "Suffer the little children to come unto me…"

Victoria's visit to Renaissance Ministries was an expression of the Kingdom of God.

I encourage you to read this book Big Angels and Flaming Wild Horses. You will not be disappointed.

If you haven't read 6 Big Angels, do so. Every chapter had me on edge just wanting to know more about my heavenly home.

This is an awesome description of the vision and visitation of little Valor Victoria. It will bless you and your ministry as it did ours.

Reverend Thierry B. Argentin
Pastor- Renaissance Church
West Palm Beach, Florida

Acknowledgements

Again, with a grateful heart, I acknowledge the efforts of our granddaughter Victoria. Without her willingness to share in detail with us her heavenly experiences, this book would not be possible.

No one, who has not experienced what she has, can understand the stress that comes with intimate encounters in the supernatural realm. Even while being harassed by demons, she has provided us with more valuable information than we can understand.

Even under the pressure, she lives up to the name God gave her, **Valor Victoria.**

To Don Pennington, Grandpa, my husband. He has guided me step by step through the struggles involved in writing this book. Even with the delays caused by my accident that resulted in a fractured pelvis, he has stood with me to do whatever was required to complete the task. My husband is unfailingly patient and has proven to be a true servant of God.

To my youngest daughter Stephanie, who without question dropped everything to fly down the next day after my accident. She gave me superb nursing care. She was my night watch angel.

To my next youngest daughter Lorri, who stepped in as my protector from the medical profession. Without her as an assisting hand to God, my healer, I could have suffered great damage.

To Leila and Tim Baldwin who without a doubt have done more to spread the word than any other two people I can name. They have been faithful to keep plenty of books on hand to give away to anyone who will receive them including Sid Roth.

To my brother in law Greg Pennington, whose hungry heart received each new update with delight and encouragement.

To Willie Richmond, our Cajun intercessor along with her two prayer partners, Jeannie and Carolyn. They have stepped in tirelessly when we needed support and encouragement.

To Ila Mae McLeighton, Pastor of El Shaddai Revival Worship Center and her Daughter Donna, for listening to the Voice of God and inviting an unknown ministry to test its wings and gain experience. We love you Ila Mae.

To Victoria's Pastor, David Garcia for embracing the truth of her experience and taking the time to know her.

There are so many others too numerous to tell. There are some we cannot fail to mention for their loyal support and encouragement. A few of them include Susan Hewlett, Sue Byington, Nancy and Tina intercessors in Baxley, Georgia, Tom and Sue Breuner, Ted Freeman and so many others we do not have room to mention. They know who they are and that we love them.

Prologue

It was September 2, 2003 when Majo slipped and accidentally knocked Victoria off the top of our swimming pool sliding board. Victoria fell backwards to the concrete deck nine feet below and was unharmed.

When she started to fall she heard God yell, "Save the children! Catch Victoria!" Then 6 Big, Big, Big Angels caught her and ZOOM, took her up to heaven.

The account of her accident is told in our first book, 6 Big Big Big Angels.

In that few seconds while she was falling, she was transported to heaven in the hands of six big, powerful and beautiful angels.

She saw a lot of heaven in that brief span of earthly time. Our count of time means nothing in the heavenly realm.

She spent some time in the Baby Place where she saw a lot of babies. Some were so tiny she could hold them in her little 41/2 year old hands.

She told Majo that these tiny babies had been "squeezed out their mommy's tummy before they were big enough to live." The reality was, these were aborted babies.

She even named some of them that she spent time with during that first visit to heaven. Some of them she named included Alcie Treehunter, Majolynn Mist and Little Victoria.

She saw some other babies that were bigger and older.

She named one of them Garbage Baby.

This little girl was born full term, and put into a garbage dumpster alive. She died on the way to the landfill in the garbage truck. The angels came and took her to heaven.

On a later visit she met a young boy she called The Teenage Boy. He played music in the Baby Place.

She saw many other children on her many visits to heaven. These are just a few examples of what she saw.

We encourage you to get a copy of 6 Big Big Big Angels and read the amazing things Victoria revealed to us about the wonders of heaven and God's Glory.

> 1 Sam 9:19
> 19 Samuel answered Saul and said, "I am the seer. Go up before me to the high place, for you shall eat with me today; and tomorrow I will let you go and will tell you all that is in your heart.
>
> 2 Kings 17:13
> 13 Yet the LORD testified against Israel and against Judah, by all of His prophets, every seer, saying, "Turn from your evil ways, and keep My commandments and My statutes, according to all the law which I commanded your fathers, and which I sent to you by My servants the prophets."
>
> 1 Chron 29:29
> 29 Now the acts of King David, first and last, indeed they are written in the book of Samuel the seer, in the book of Nathan the prophet, and in the book of Gad the seer,

A TALK BETWEEN US SEERS

In January 2005 during the annual convening of International Apostolic Ministries (IAM), we were blessed to have Pat Holloran[1] as a guest in our home. He was one of the speakers for the meetings.

Pat and his wife Valeria are Seers and Prophets. We had never met them. The host church just assigned them to us.

This is an account of a conversation between Pat and Victoria while he was with us.

What Pat shared with Victoria provided very sound and important instruction and teaching for her.

We believe that this time with Pat and Valeria gave her the confidence to walk in the gifts God gave her.

What a God given blessing that experience was! Victoria and Pat have become very close.

The first day they were here, Pat sat on the couch beside Victoria and started to talk to her. He told her that the bible tells about people that were prophets. But they became Seers before they became prophets. He wanted to be sure she understood what he was saying.

> 1 Sam 9:9
> 9Formerly in Israel, when a man went to inquire of God, he spoke thus: "Come, let us go to the seer"; for he who is now called a prophet was formerly called a seer.

He told Victoria that he was what is called a Seer. Then He said that she was a Seer too.

---

[1] Pastors Pat and Valeria Holloran
Harvest House International Ministries, Inc.
P O Box 28083
Bellingham, WA 98228
www.patholloran.com

He went on to encourage her, even at this early age, to learn the word of God so she did not always have to see all the bad stuff.

He related that at one time he even wondered where all the angels went.

He was just seeing the bad stuff like demons. They can do all sorts of stuff to frighten us because they know who we are and they know we can see them.

Victoria told him that she tells them, "In the name of Jesus, you have to go."

He instructed her that when she tells them to go, she should say to them "Go under the feet of Jesus Christ" according to Ephesians, chapter 1. When we read that scripture, the Holy Spirit tells us what they are.

> Eph 1:22-23
> 22 And He put all things under His feet, and gave Him to be head over all things to the church,

Victoria told him that she saw demons when she was up in heaven. She saw one that said, "AHAAA... AHHHAAA."

She was really talking about the living creatures and not demons. They make a very loud powerful sound as they move and breathe.

For a long time she was not sure what they were. Victoria had told us earlier that she had seen demons when she went into the throne room.

One was a lion. One was an eagle. One was a cow and the other one was a man. They had lots of eyes.

It was almost a year later that she finally realized that the living creatures were the Good Guys. She described them as having "lots of faces on thur face."

She did not fully understand what Pat meant when he confirmed what she saw. They were the four living creatures. They have eyes in their wings and eyes on their bodies because they see everything.

They go wherever God looks. So when you see the four living creatures then you know God has looked at you.

Pat encouraged Victoria by telling her that he did not want her to ever lose this gift.

Unfortunately many seers have given up their gift because they were discouraged or afraid.

He assured her that being a seer was going to be really good and she should not be afraid because fear is not of God.

He warned her that people like her and him and Valeria can never afford to be discouraged. They have to believe that everything is OK even when times are tough.

He assured her that all seers do not always see the same things all the time but that was OK. The bible says, "We see in part so we prophesy in part."

There will be times when she sees angels that other seers do not see. There are going to be times that someone else sees something that she does not see.

Seers have to show each other sometimes because that's the way the prophetic works.

Pat told her she may not understand these words right now, but in the future, she will.

He said to her, "Because I know I will see you again. I know I'll be here next year."

He encouraged her when he told her that he would definitely be seeing her again soon.

He wants to keep an eye on her to see how she is doing. He wants to watch her grow.

Victoria has not seen the last of her favorite Seer.

CHAPTER 1

DESTINY DOORS OPEN

AWESOME NIGHT

Things started with a bang as the music carried us into powerful praise and worship by a band called "Judah."[2] God moved in power. We were swept up into the Glory.

The next morning, Victoria casually said, "Last night was awesome."

Sandi asked what she saw and she replied, "That place was full of huge angels that came pouring in as soon as the music started."

Sandi asked if she saw anything else and she nodded and said, "Yep. Wild horses with fire all over them was running all through the people. Everywhere the wild horses ran, it caused flaming tornados"

She explained later that the tornados are "fire that comes from the fiery horses."

Victoria had mentioned seeing angels before, but this was the first time she mentioned the Flaming Wild Horses.

---

[2] Judah
Ryan Ballard
P.O. Box 75222
Salem, MI 48175

We were excited and wondered what it meant.

NASHVILLE, TENNESSEE

Jeff Jansen, founder of Global Fire Ministries[3] was the sponsor of the Destiny Doors Conference.

We met Jeff at the filming for Sid Roth's "It's Supernatural" TV show in June 2006.

Later Jeff and Jan invited us to participate in this conference.

It was held in a huge warehouse that had been part of an auto works. It had big wooden front doors with rounded tops that looked like they belonged in a castle. The sign at the entrance read, "DESTINY DOORS."

The buildings are over 100 years old. It houses an outreach ministry of provision, faith and love and is located right in the heart of a section of Nashville that really needs love.

Friday night was great and Victoria again saw big angels and lots of wild horses covered in flames.

SLATTERED BY BANDALS

Saturday we were scheduled to be the first to speak at the 2:00 PM service. Just before the service started, Grandpa and Sandi went to the back of the building to get something out of the Suburban and found one of the windows had been broken.

Sandi stayed with the car and Grandpa ran back around

---

[3] Jeff Jansen
Global Fire Ministries
615-867-1124
www.globalfireministries.com

front and told us, “The car has been vandalized. The window has been shattered. The car next to ours was hit by vandals, too.”

Someone walked up and asked what happened and Victoria explained, “The car got ‘banded’ and the window got ‘slattered’ by ‘bandals’. That other car beside us got ‘bandeded’, too.”

Grandpa was detained around back with the police when we were supposed to speak and Sandi came back around front to be with Victoria.

Jeff asked me to come forward and insisted that Sandi and Victoria come on up also. Up to that point they had not come to the front in a service. Sandi had always kept Victoria protected and in the back of the auditorium.

I was excited. When I got up to speak that day, September 2nd 2006, it was the anniversary of the *exact time* and date of Victoria’s fall from our slide, three years earlier. That event and her trip to heaven is what changed our lives forever.

Jeff handed me the microphone and I started with, “Three years ago today Victoria took a fall that should have been fatal...

We told the people about Victoria’s fall and the 6 Big Angels. Then we briefly told them about heaven, and the aborted babies and how the babies forgive and love their mommies.

The Holy Spirit anointed the words that came out of my mouth as I spoke. When I finished people were yelling... More! We want to hear more! Tell us more!

Sharnael Wolverton of Swiftfire Ministries International came up to Jeff and said “Let them continue to speak. This is anointed. Can't you feel that the faith level has been raised 100% in this room while they talked?"

Jeff asked me to tell about the Flaming Wild Horses that Victoria saw the first night of the conference and about my dream of Israel.

As I told about the Horses I could feel waves of Glory flowing over me.

When we finished again, Sharnael came up and asked Jeff to let us pray impartation over them.

There was no more time. They had other speakers scheduled and were on a tight schedule.

I was glad he didn't ask us to do a prayer of impartation because I wouldn't have known what to say. I didn't know how to do that.

As soon as the service ended, people lined up at our book table wanting prayer for impartation.

Sharnael, who wanted us to tell more about heaven, was the first person to come and ask us to pray impartation over her.

I said, "My dear, I am just a grandmother and I really don't know how to do this... but I will ask God to do it.

So I prayed for her and asked God to look and see the hunger in her heart and to open her eyes and impart the ability to see into the supernatural and open her nose so she could smell the fragrance of heaven and open her ears that she would hear the slightest whisper from Him.

As we prayed for the people, many immediately saw angels. Some could describe them in vivid detail.

Some saw the flaming horses and others even heard them.

Four ladies came up who had heard the hoof beats, the heavy breathing and the mighty heartbeat of the huge Flaming Wild Horses.

Many people that we prayed for instantly saw into the heavens. I was astonished! They could see more than I could!

At one point as we prayed in a circle for four people they all saw angels throwing silver coins and showering us with golden glitter.

A man that we had just prayed for saw an angel ministering with me that had green gems all over him.

We prayed for people all afternoon. We stopped just in time to get a drink of water and find some food and an apple for Victoria to eat before the evening service started.

GREAT CROWD OF WITNESSES

The evening service was entirely awesome. Once again, Judah carried us up with the music. The praise and worship leader, Ryan said, “We are singing to a dual audience; the physical audience and the spiritual audience.”

We had an open heaven and were surrounded by the Great Cloud of Witnesses.

Victoria said she saw a great ***crowd*** of people from heaven. Spirits, not living people. “They used to be people but they are not people anymore because they are spirits.”

CORONATION OF KING OVER NASHVILLE

Then Randy Demain came up to speak. He read Psalm 24, and told us we were the gates and we were going to have a coronation of Jesus Christ the King.

THE EARTH IS HIS

Psalm 24:1, 3, 4, 5, 6, 7-10
1 The earth belongs to the Lord,
and everything in it...
the world and all it's people.
3 Who may go up on the mountain of the Lord?
Who may stand in His Holy Temple?

CLEAN HANDS, PURE HEART

4 Only those with clean hands and pure hearts...
5 They will receive a blessing from the Lord;
The God who saves them will declare them right.
6 They try to follow God;
They look to the God of Jacob for help.

OPEN UP, YE GATES

Gates, open all the way.
Open wide, aged doors
so the glorious king will come in.
8 Who is this glorious King?

THE LORD, MIGHTY WARRIOR

The Lord, strong and mighty.
The Lord, the powerful warrior.
9 Gates, open all the way.
Open wide, aged doors
so the glorious King will come in.

THE LORD, ALL POWERFUL

10 Who is this glorious King?
The Lord All-Powerful
He is the glorious King.
The Youth Bible, New Century Version

KING JESUS

As we went through the Psalm and praised, we felt the mighty presence of King Jesus. You could feel His Majesty and Glory as He swept down the aisle in His Magnificent Robe. It was glorious.

During the time of seating the King and on into the awesome time of worship, everyone was singing and praising in one mind and one accord. The musicians and the singers and the audience were in perfect unity.

I kept seeing whirlwinds on the stage.

At one point a girl's flag was spinning in the shape of a tornado. It was because of one of these whirlwinds.

I saw a lot of golden haze and sometimes green haze or clouds. Then the clouds would change colors to amber.

WHEN THE SINGERS

> 2 Chron 5:12-14
> 12 and the Levites who were the singers,
> all those of Asaph and Heman and Jeduthun, with their sons and their brethren, stood at the east end of the altar, clothed in white linen,

AND MUSICIANS

> having cymbals, stringed instruments and harps, and with them one hundred and twenty priests sounding with trumpets

WERE AS ONE

> 13 indeed it came to pass, when the trumpeters and singers were as one, to make one sound to be heard in praising and thanking the LORD, and when they lifted

up their voice with the trumpets and cymbals and instruments of music,

AND PRAISED THE LORD IN SONG

and praised the LORD, saying: "For He is good,
For His mercy endures forever,"

A CLOUD OF GLORY FILLED THE HOUSE

that the house, the house of the LORD, was filled with a cloud,
14 so that the priests could not continue ministering
because of the cloud; for the glory of the LORD filled the
house of God.

A LIVING TRUMPET

When we were all shouting and lifting up our voices to heaven, my mouth became a trumpet. I felt the flared horn part of the trumpet stretching my mouth into a big circle and I felt the golden metal around the inside of my lips. I could even taste the metal in my mouth.

I looked across from me and a lady standing just in front of the stage turned toward me. I was surprised to see that her mouth was also a large circle like a trumpet. When she saw me… her eyes stretched large in surprise.

I literally felt like I was a large living trumpet and I could see my "sound" like a ribbon coming out of my mouth and curling upward.

PORTABLE THRONE

The heavens were open and I could see this ribbon of praise go all the way to God's Throne.

I could see the throne just over the top of the building, there was a glowing, and shining. I could see fire and smoke and lightening but I could not see God's face, just the shining.

It was His portable throne. Victoria and I both saw it.

A CROWN FOR JESUS

Victoria actually saw what the rest of us could only feel. She told me that she saw Jesus the King as He came down the aisle. He went up on the stage and sat down on a beautiful throne. A crown was placed on His head by two smaller angels.

The angels the night before had been huge so these two seemed smaller but were probably about 8 feet tall.

She could look up and see God watching from His throne just above the building.

BREAKTHROUGH ANGEL

Then she said, "This really huge angel comed in that was beautiful and shiny."

This "shiny" angel is the one Randy was waiting for, Breakthrough Angel.

She saw the Flaming Wild Horses galloping through the crowd again as they had done on the first night.

God came down from His throne and danced with Victoria and the people. The four faces were there... moving swiftly from side to side.

Victoria had first seen the living creatures here in the earth, when we were having dinner with Sid Roth, one night during the filming of the Sid Roth TV program.

A NIGHT TO REMEMBER

It was a night to remember. People were laying face down

all over. Many were drunk in the spirit and couldn't walk.

Sandi kept popping from one side of the aisle to the other as though she was a rubber ball and someone had just hit her with a bat.

I staggered back toward the table, only to be knocked down by the power of God as someone accidentally brushed against me. I finally crawled on all fours to a chair and pulled myself up.

With great care, I walked back to the book table. People were already coming and asking for prayers of impartation.

This was a day to remember. It was three years since Victoria fell off the slide and went to heaven.

It was her third anniversary and we crowned Jesus Christ, King of Kings and Lord of Lords of Nashville, Tennessee.

The next morning we came down to the breakfast bar of the hotel. People from the conference who were staying there asked for prayers of impartation in front of the coffee machine and others caught up with us in front of the elevator.

FIRST REPORT

After we arrived home, I was writing Jan Jansen about some of the supernatural things that Victoria and I saw in Nashville and Victoria came and asked me to read it.

After I read it to her she asked if she could type a message to Jeff and Jan.

She sat on my knee and laboriously typed with one finger the first written report she has ever given.

dear Jeff and Jan and mercy,
I saw a tornado too. And god and Jesus. 4 flags swirling. 2 little angels and God's throne. Jesus on his throne with a crown on his head up on the stage. and the big beautiful angel called breakthrough came in and was really huge. there was wild horses with fire.

love,
Victoria

FLASH! LAST MINUTE UPDATE!

Recently, as we were trying to finish this book, "Big Angels and Flaming Wild Horses", Sandi, Grandpa and I were discussing the Nashville conference and how the faith level had risen as we told about the Glory of heaven.

After Jeff asked us to tell the people about the Flaming Wild Horses, the faith level went up even higher. We were aware that it was happening but did not understand what had allowed it. When we prayed a prayer of impartation for people after the service, many began to see into the spirit realm.

After our discussion, we went to bed, but Victoria still had something to tell her Mommy. She told Sandi that as we talk about the Glory and the horses, more things happen. When we talk about heaven and the Glory, more Glory comes. She told her mother, "As you talked about the Wild Horses in Nashville, more came bustin' in and so people believed more."

She summed up, "The more you talk about Big Angels and Flaming Wild Horses in the services, the more Holy the service becomes and the more Holy the new book becomes." *I believe she meant anointed when she said "Holy."*

What we experienced in Nashville began to make more sense to us. Sometimes, we are slow learners.

She told us the place was full of huge angels that came pouring in when the music started. Then the Flaming Wild Horses came in as the people praised and worshipped God on that first night.

They were there but nobody knew about them. We tried to tell someone about them but the word did not get out.

The point is, the Flaming Wild Horses were there for five services and nobody knew about them. When we spoke about heaven at the 2:00 PM service, the Glory was imparted to the congregation and the faith level built, but I ended without telling about the horses, because I did not understand what the Flaming Wild Horses really are.

However, by this time, word of the horses had reached Jeff, but like us he did not realize what they represented. He asked me to tell them about the horses. He thought they were connected to the history of the area when a band of wild horses ran about the territory during the early days of settlement in America.

As Victoria told us later, when I began to tell about the Flaming Wild Horses, more came "bustin'" in.

The people who asked for prayer and impartation after the meeting received because the Fire of the Holy Spirit (Flaming Wild Horses and Whirlwinds) was completely filling the building.

I believe the Flaming Wild Horses represent The Third Person of the Godhead, Holy Ghost, who has burst out of the box and is running free. As we speak of Him... we receive more of His Fire and Glory.

As we speak about the Glory of God, we increase our ***knowledge*** of His Glory. Then, "The knowledge of the glory of God will cover the earth as the waters cover the sea." Habakkuk 2:14

CHAPTER 2

LOUISIANA CONNECTION

WAY DOWN YONDER

After we got home from the conference in Nashville we received a call from Sharnael Wolverton of Swiftfire Ministries International.

She had read the book, 6 Big Angels on the plane. She had a lay over in an airport and finished it. It spoke to her in so many ways. She cried all the way home.

Sharnael was kind and sent me a letter about how she felt after we spoke at Nashville and what happened as she read our book.

SEEDS OF JUSTICE

By Sharnael Wolverton

After meeting Mary Jo, Don, Sandi and Victoria and hearing their testimony, I was moved to tears.

I, too, had experienced seeing glimpses of heaven regarding these babies and regarding my own two baby girls that had gone to be with Jesus.

I even have a teaching I released many times regarding the things the Lord showed me during my grieving process: "Moving from Shaking to Ground Breaking."

The Lord called these little ones "Seeds of Justice."

Until that day, I had only heard of one other person who had shared openly any revelation regarding this subject so it was beyond comforting to be able to meet them, hear more and exchange revelations.

Victoria saw and understood many more wonderful things than I ever did. It filled my heart with great joy, peace, understanding and comfort to be able to read her book on the plane ride home.

As I read and cried I could feel the presence of the girls as they came and sat in the empty seat beside me. They were so tiny. I felt so much love

NOT JUST A GRANDMOTHER

When she got home, Sharnael called me and said, "When you prayed for me in Nashville you said, 'I'm not sure how to do this, I am just an old grandmother.'"

She continued, "Never say that again. You are a powerful woman of God. You are more than a conqueror. You are special to God."

Then she told me that she used to say, "I'm just a baby prophet," but Jim Sky a prophet of God, set her straight.

NOT A BABY PROPHET

Jim said to her, "You are not a baby prophet. You are a prophet, called of God. Never say that again."

Now she was giving me that same advice.

COME TO LOUISIANA

She was holding an AmpliFIRE conference in Baton Rouge, Louisiana, less than three weeks after the Nashville meetings. She asked if we could come on short notice to speak.

We checked our calendar and Sandi's work schedule and saw we would be able to make it. We called her back and accepted the invitation.

GOD SENT INTERCESSORS

Willie Richmond, an intercessor from Lake Charles, Louisiana had ordered the 6 Big Angels book when we were on the way home from a ministry trip. We misplaced her order.

She called to let us know she had not received her book and she really needed it.

She had borrowed a girl's book and kept it. The girl kept calling and wanting her book back. Willie just couldn't give it back until she received her own copy from us.

Then her daughter had a miscarriage and Willie knew why she had kept the book. She and her daughter read about the Baby Place, about Jesus making the babies well and the babies' rooms. They read to each other. It helped them make it through this very sad time of losing their precious baby. We immediately sent her some books.

When I realized we were going to be in Louisiana, I called Willie and asked her to come to Baton Rouge.

BATON ROUGE

Grandpa, Victoria and I drove to Baton Rouge and arrived there Thursday afternoon.

As soon as we got to the conference on Thursday night, I asked Victoria to look inside the sanctuary and see what was in there.

She checked it out and came back and reported that there were a lot of big angels there and the Healing angel was already there.

The praise music started and it was awesome. I asked Victoria if she saw anything else. She answered yes; the Flaming Wild Horses were running through the people and as they ran, whirlwinds of fire were spinning off them.

Saturday afternoon Victoria said the healing angel and the big angels were still there and the flaming wild horses were there.

Grandpa, Sandi, Victoria and I slipped into a small room and repeated together our declaration of unity three times, "AS ONE!"

Lance Walnau[4] had taught on Unity the night before and taught us to declare it into the atmosphere that we four are **as one**.

Something happens in the heavens when two or more people make that declaration of unity from the heart.

TAKE US TO THE THRONE

Sandi began the service with prayer. When Sandi prays from her pure heart, it brings the anointing. She took us right before God.

We gave the testimony of Victoria's fall and experiences in heaven and I told some of the precious things that Victoria told us for the children's books. She has given some little details that were not in the first book, "6 Big Angels."

We told how God and His throne had been at Nashville. That was where we first saw the Flaming Wild Horses and fiery whirlwinds.

---

[4] Lance Wallnau
Lance Wallnau Ministries
1308 Phoenix Ave.
Cranston, Rhode Island 02921
www.lancelearning.com

Victoria has now explained that when the praise and worship begins, the Flaming Wild Horses come into the building. She told us that as we speak about them, more and more horses arrive. The more we recognize them and talk about them, the more they come.

It is as if the Holy Spirit has burst out of the box and is running free among us.

In closing, we prayed a prayer of impartation over the congregation. Sharnael asked if we were willing to pray for people and we said we would be happy to do that.

People came forward and formed three separate lines in front of Sandi, Grandpa and me.

When we started to pray, things began to happen. People were seeing whirlwinds, Flaming Wild Horses and angels. Some were healed. Some were just lying on the floor in the presence of God.

Many people would go from one line to another for prayer from each one of us.

During the ministry time, Willie and our two other intercessor friends, Carolyn Richard and Jeannie George, were right behind us praying for our feet and supplying us with water.

We ministered until it was time for the 7:00 PM meeting to start.

Without delay Sharnael went right into the evening service. Once again the music was awesome and what was in the natural moved into the Supernatural.

WILD HORSES

Two prophetic artists were painting as we sang and danced, during praise and worship. It was fascinating to watch as the paintings progressed from service to service. We had not even noticed that one of them had begun to paint a horse in the afternoon service.

Victoria saw a lot of things in the spirit during the music and throughout the meeting. She saw the Flaming Wild Horses running through the people. Whirlwinds were spinning off them.

The drums were really beating loudly and Sandi started clapping her hands and stomping her feet to the beat. Other people began to join in. It was like we were swept up by the heartbeat of God

WAR DANCE

It started to sound like a war dance. Victoria saw heavenly Indians dancing warfare in the spirit.

As we were dancing I looked over at the painting by one of the prophetic artists, Maylia Trahan.[5] She was painting wild horses on the canvas. She had been working on the painting since the meetings began on Thursday.

The artist later told us that she heard the hoof beats of the horses while she was painting that night.

Jim Sky, a prophet and an American Indian, stood up and gave a wonderful prophetic word to the people.

FOUR FACES AND GOD'S THRONE

Victoria saw many other things that night. She saw the "Four Faces." That is what she calls the Living Creatures. They were moving real fast.

---

[5] Maylia G. Trahan
Prophetic Artist
Baton Rouge, LA
www.restorehearts.com

God was dancing with the people up front. God's throne was just above the building. Jesus came down from His throne on the stage and danced with the people.

GABRIEL AND MICHAEL

Gabriel was there on a huge horse on one side of Sharnael. Michael was on a huge horse on the other side of her.

Everywhere Sharnael moved; they would move with her and always stayed right beside her.

COP ANGELS

Michael's warriors were with him. Victoria told us that the building was surrounded on the inside by "Cop Angels" standing shoulder to shoulder.

She first saw the Cop Angels at a church in Winter Haven, Florida just a few weeks after she fell and went to heaven in 2003.

Those meetings in Winter Haven were awesome. An anointed prophet, Glenn Miller,[6] was teaching on the Calendar of God. We went to the meetings all week. He was the first to teach us about The Feast of Trumpets, Rosh Hashanah… with the cop angels in attendance.

I was so impressed by this new knowledge as we learned about the days of awe, that I wanted to immediately go back to our home church on Sunday and tell the people about the importance of recognizing God's calendar.

I even called all our children and explained it to them. I

---

[6] Glenn Miller
Lions Share Ministries
4600 Mobile Highway
Suite 9, Box 351
Pensacola, FL 32506

asked them to repent if they had anything in their life that was not pleasing to God, because the next day was Yom Kippur... the Day of Atonement.

What happened to Victoria in those services in Winter Haven was related in the first book 6 Big Angels. She called the warriors Cop Angels because they had "swords and spears and things to fight with."

Little did we know that God was just beginning to lead us into a greater understanding of His ways and His Glory.

Here we were in Baton Rouge during another Feast of Trumpets and Michael and the cop angels were with us again.

NO DEMONS LEFT

The Flaming Wild Horses and the Cop Angels had removed all of the demons that may have tried to disrupt the meetings.

Victoria told us, "One small demon tried to sneak back into the building up in the corner behind the drums… and one of the horses ran toward him and 'Zoop!'... he goed right back out through the wall!"

I believe it is significant that the most persistent demon who tried to get back in was after the drummer. If he could have attacked and distracted the drummer... the rhythm of the worship could have been disrupted.

I believe that there is a strong anointing on drummers in this season to feel the heart beat of God and play it on their drums.

I believe Gabriel came that night because a message of world portent was delivered to Sharnael. I believe Michael came to protect the message.

A lot of things began to happen to her after that.

Remember her name. When Gabriel delivers the message, it is important.

Sharnael let us know what has happened in the natural because of her encounter with Gabriel and Michael. The following is her account.

THE RESPONSE IN THE NATURAL TO A SUPERNATURAL ENCOUNTER

There were many important things that happened as a result of the encounter with Gabriel and Michael that night on September 23, 2006. There may be more things that continue to unfold but these things happened almost immediately!

Within three weeks of the encounter, on October 17, 2006, I was pregnant (in the natural) with a baby girl. This baby was especially important to me because I had just gone through two miscarriages in less than two years time.

I had received several words spoken over me concerning this child and now here was my baby, a special child with the due date of 07-07-07.

I found out I was pregnant because an angel came to me in the night of October 27, 2006 and said "You're pregnant."

I instantly thought about the last two miscarriages. I must have looked fearful as she delivered the message.

She immediately held up her hand and said, "No. Don't worry; I am here to help you." And then she was gone.

The next day my six-year old, Shaen, came home from school with a picture she had colored of an angel pushing a stroller. The stroller was colored in the same colors as our stroller in real life. I had only shared the information about the baby with my husband! Someone had told her too!

This kind of angel activity, I believe, is a direct result of Mary Jo praying for me in Nashville. I have had many encounters to speak of but they have increased significantly since I was able to have her pray for me!

Another interesting thing that happened was we received a call from an International Christian Network regarding starting our own Christian Television show.

This is something I laughed about when I first received the call. I had never imagined or even desired to do anything even close. But I was quickly rebuked by the Lord.

He reminded me of my hearts cry for nations and revival. I had prayed and cried many tears, many years for nations. This was the avenue HE was choosing.

Within 24 hours of receiving that call, a stranger emailed and offered free services for producing if we ever needed it. She had a producing and directing background and said that if something like that ever came up for us that she felt she was to help us!

She was not even aware we had a Television offer but had come to the same meeting at which Mary Jo, Don, Sandi and Victoria spoke in September.

Many, many supernatural things like this lined up in order for this to happen.

But the bottom line is, we now have a weekly national television program called "Swiftfire with Sharnael Wolverton" with plans to go international.

"God TV" has also offered to air our conferences internationally at no cost to the ministry! We have had a total of three networks now offering us air time.

Gabriel brings global message and commission, Michael comes to protect it!

The last thing that happened to me and the ministry is a reawakening for a book the Lord had given me back in 2004.

The title is "Key to Third Heaven… Using Third Heaven Revelation to Impact a World." The manuscript was written in 2004 but the warfare to get it published was so difficult that frankly, I just couldn't go any further.

I had trouble in every direction trying to get it edited, designed and published. Then, without notice, I received two emails from two different people offering services to edit for me. They didn't even know I had written anything.

But again, people were offering services for future projects!

This jump started my heart to move forward! The grace was suddenly there and the people were there to help me!

Don Pennington even offered to do the layout and formatting of the book for me!

We had decided to self publish and in the midst I even had an international publisher offer me a three book deal! She had never even met me or read anything I ever wrote.

We decided not to go this way because we felt the Lord was asking US to publish and start our own publishing house but it gave me confirmation that we were definitely on the right track!

Since then, the Lord has given me a second book, "Seers Handbook" and two others I am currently working on. The revelation continues!

If these things do not display favor and life changing shifts that will rock your socks off, I don't know what could!?

I know I have a lot of exclamation marks following the sentences written above but I am so excited that I am shouting with delight over what the Lord has done so quickly!

God is so amazing!

Sharnael Wolverton,
Swiftfire Ministries International

As God continues to lead us and bless Victoria, we continually gain more knowledge of heaven and its Glory.

CHAPTER 3

TUPELO & BEYOND

We left Baton Rouge early Sunday morning and headed for Tupelo, Mississippi, to speak that evening.

Sheryl Trayler called me about a week before we went to Baton Rouge. She had read the book and wanted to know what it would take to get us to Tupelo. I asked how far they were from Baton Rouge and she told me about 7 hours. I didn't hesitate, I said if you have church on Sunday night we can get there. We'll just drive from Baton Rouge.

Sheryl and Terry Trayler pastor a small congregation in a storefront church, called LIFE CHANGING MINISTRIES.[7]

On the way to Tupelo, Victoria got her pencils and paper and started to draw. She drew a wild horse and then she drew something coming out of his mouth. When she showed it to us we asked her what the stuff was coming out of its mouth. She told us it was fire balls.

I asked her, "What is the purpose of the fireballs?"

She said, "It makes the demons run. It scares them real bad. They go right through the wall and leave the building."

---

[7] Life Changing Ministries
146 E. Thomas Street, Suite E
Tupelo, Mississippi, 38801
Phone 662-871-0327

She told us again, that the night before in Baton Rouge, a demon tried to sneak back in on the platform behind the drums. One of those wild horses spit a fire ball at him and he ducked right back out through the wall of the building and POW! ... he was gone.

Then she drew a shield held by an angel with Sandi behind it. The shield had jagged lines like lightning coming out the front and I asked her what it was.

She said, "Well, that is like power and lightning of God. It shoots out from the shield."

When I asked her what the power did she replied, "It makes the demons weak and they fall to the ground."

This is when I realized that our shield of faith is an OFFENSIVE weapon as well as a defensive weapon.

We made it to the church with a few minutes to spare.

The church had only a few members then, but Sheryl had advertised that we were coming and the church was full.

Victoria sat with us as we sang praises and worshiped the Lord.

Terry turned the service over to us and Sandi ushered in the anointing when she prayed.

Grandpa spoke first with the introduction. Then I spoke telling some of the details of Victoria's experiences in heaven.

Victoria was showing the audience some of her drawings of the shield of faith and the Flaming Wild Horses as we spoke. The Lord was beginning to move her out among the people.

I asked Sandi to come to the microphone and tell what we call the Bedtime Stories. Sandi had always stayed in the background before, but on this trip, God was pulling her out.

FIRST SPOKEN PROPHETIC WORD

As Sandi was speaking, Victoria came to the podium, reached for the microphone and said, "I have something to say."

We were astonished! Victoria had always stayed either sitting in the back of the church or lying on a quilt under a pew. Apparently, God was pulling her out, too.

She turned to Pastors Terry and Sheryl and began to speak. She told them, "You are going to have 1000 people."

She dropped her head and closed her eyes. Then she raised her head and continued to speak to the Pastors. "No. God said you are going to have ***2000*** people and you are going to need to build a big church to hold all the people. This church is too little. You are going to have lots of money and you are going to travel around the world."

There was excitement among the congregation. Some of them told Sandi that just the week before, by faith, they had paid down on a piece of property.

Needless to say Terry and Sheryl were excited by the time Victoria finished giving her first public prophetic word.

The Feast of Trumpets ended at sundown and the Days of Awe were beginning.

We don't understand the timing of God yet, but I know His timing had something to do with her stepping forward with a public prophetic word, at this time and in this place.

We prayed a prayer of impartation over the congregation and closed the service.

As we talked to Sheryl after the service, she confirmed that just four days before, they had paid down on a piece of property to build a new church.

We went back to the pastor's house and had already gone upstairs to go to bed, when I suddenly realized that I had not turned my mobile phone back on. When I turned it on there was a message waiting for me.

A girl named Regina had called and said, "Majo, this is Regina. Please call me. There is a BIG ANGEL on my car!"

I ran back downstairs and knocked on the door of Sheryl's bedroom. I said, "Sheryl, come out I need to talk to you."

She came out and asked me if something was wrong.

I asked her if she knew Regina and she told me that she does know her, she was at church that night.

I said, "Regina has an angel on her car."

Sheryl exclaimed, "Say what? An Angel on her car?"

I called Regina and she told me what happened.

She said she left the service believing that she was going to see angels. As she parked the car, went up the walk, and opened her door she expected to see angels in her apartment.

She had just walked in her front door and her phone rang. Her mother who lived down the street in another apartment was calling to ask Regina to come down and sign some papers for her brother.

Regina picked up her keys, went out the door and locked it. As she turned around and started walking down the sidewalk toward the street, she glanced up and saw a huge Angel on the hood of her car.

She tried to call her mother on her mobile phone, but it would not work. She started screaming and her nephew came out of one of the apartments down the other way. She sent him to get her mother.

Others found out and many people were coming out of the apartments. They all saw the angel. There were two angels at the back of her car that were smaller than the one on the hood of the car.

Regina called later and told me the angels stayed there all night.

Everybody could see the angels; saint and sinner alike.

I believe God has stretched out His hand and touched Tupelo, Mississippi to raise up a group of His people to usher in the next mighty move of God.

TUPELO UPDATE

The pastor's wife wrote later and told me some of the things that have happened since we were there.

> *By Sheryl Traylor*
>
> *Back in September when you came to visit our church, Victoria spoke the word of prophecy to us about the church growth that was coming.*
>
> *She said that thousands of people would be coming and we would have to get a bigger church.*
>
> *Well, since that date we have had that spoken to us on several different occasions.*

About three weeks after you left, my mother passed away. I couldn't understand how that could happen without God really showing me that it was going to happen. But God told me He took her because she was ready to come home.

Well, the night before she passed, we had visitors that came from Johnstown, Pennsylvania. They had never been to Mississippi before.

They hardly knew us. In fact, they had only seen us one time before this visit.

They said that God had sent them there to give us a prophetic word.

They told us the same thing that Victoria prophesied. They said there would be many people coming to the church.

They told us that some changes would take place first.

The next afternoon while they were still here, my mother called and said that she had fallen and needed us to come and help her. I rushed to her house and she died only fifteen minutes later.

The next couple of days, God let me know what he was doing. He let me know that my mother's death was the beginning of the fulfillment of the prophetic word Victoria had spoken on that Sunday in September.

Her death and funeral was the beginning of the things that were about to happen for the growth to take place.

Since we are a storefront church at this present time, we had to have her funeral at the church where my mother grew up.

My husband does not belong to a large denominational

organization. Many of the pastors around here had never heard him preach. He eulogized my mother and the faithfulness of God as he spoke.

The word that God gave him to speak caused others to pay close attention to what God was saying for this season, and what He was about to do in the days we were about to walk through.

Since that day, some of the people who were there have come to our church because of hearing that message. One of our ministers spoke and said that God had shown her in a dream that many people would be coming because of my mother's death.

In February, we went to Canton, Georgia. A minister from Baltimore, Maryland spoke the same word to us that Victoria had spoken, when she said that this church is too small, you are going to have to get a bigger one.

He also told us that the church that we were thinking about building was too small and he hasn't, to this day seen the plans.

POWER OF PROPHETIC WORDS

I told Sheryl God has seen the plans. ***He*** has a better plan. When I talked to Sheryl recently she said that many people have come over the last eight months. Their church is experiencing supernatural growth.

Prophetic words spoken into the atmosphere bring about change. When God's word is spoken, it will come to pass because God's word cannot return void.

Victoria drew a picture of the open bible with a huge head coming out of the bible. She said, "That is God and God ***is*** the Word."

TO QUOTE TODD

Grandpa and I attended a Todd Bentley conference in Toronto, called School of the Supernatural. During that conference he quoted Psalm 103:20 and then taught us the following awesome secrets of the Word.

> Psalm 103:20
> You who are His angels, praise the Lord.
> You are the mighty warriors who do what He says.
> The Youth Bible, New Century Version

Todd said, "The angels heed the voice of His word.

"There is something about when we make a prophetic decree and declare, 'As it is in heaven.' Heaven shows up here.

"There is something about speaking the invisible in the natural that releases the invisible for people in the natural to encounter it.

"Like the testimony of Jesus with the spirit of prophecy. Sharing experiences is actually a decree.

"It is actually declaring it and the angels heed the voice of His word.

"When you speak what God says, the angels hear that, and they respond to God's word in *your* mouth. The angels also do ***His*** word. ***He*** speaks *they* respond.

"We speak, the *angels heed* to the voice, as *we* echo back what God is saying."

LEAVING TUPELO

The next morning we went back to Baton Rouge Airport to drop Sandi Off. She was flying home because she had to work on Tuesday. We drove through New Orleans and kept driving until we got to Mississippi and found a hotel close to Gulfport.

The next day we took the Coastal Highway along the Gulf of Mexico. The evidence of the devastation from hurricane Katrina was still visible. You could see the foundations of homes and businesses that had been totally destroyed.

It was a bright, clear, peaceful day and the Gulf was very calm without any waves. Victoria was looking out the window at the water.

Suddenly she excitedly said, “Look Majo! There is Jesus riding on His beautiful white horse! He is leading two of my horses from heaven; my white one and my black one!”

I was searching the horizon of the Gulf saying, “Lord, let me see! Let me see!” I didn’t see Jesus on His beautiful white horse but every time I closed my eyes, I could envision it.

RENAISSANCE CHURCH – WEST PALM BEACH

Right after we got home from Vermont and before we went to Nashville, we received a phone call from Pastor Thierry Argentin of the Renaissance Church in West Palm Beach, Florida. He invited us to speak at his church.

Pastor Argentin said that he had received a phone call from his former pastor in Norwalk, Connecticut. Pastor De Witt Stevens of the Macedonia Ministries had been using our book, Six Big Angels as a handbook to teach about heaven and angels. They were beginning to break out in revival.

IMPARTATION AND HEALING ANGEL

We began by telling about Victoria’s fall from the swimming pool sliding board and how 6 big angels caught her and took her to heaven.

We told about our experiences in other churches and the impartation by God for the people.

We prayed impartation over this audience to see into the supernatural realm of God and have dreams and visions from God.

When the pastor asked if anyone wanted prayer, almost the entire congregation crowded to the front.

Sandi, Grandpa and I began to pray for all who wanted prayer. After receiving prayer, no one went back to their seats. They stayed until all three of us had prayed for them.

Some wanted salvation. Others wanted healing and almost everyone wanted to see into the supernatural.

One lady who was visiting the church said to me, "I see things when I stand beside you. Is that alright?"

When I asked what she saw, she replied, "Do you see that old man on crutches? There is a little girl kneeling down and praying for his feet and legs. When I move away from you, I don't see her"

I told her that it was all right. That Is "Little Victoria, from heaven," she travels with us.

Victoria told us that the healing angel was there. She said. "The healing angel is HUGE! He can put his arms around *everybody* at once

BREAKTHROUGH ANGEL

Later we attended a conference in Titusville, Florida. Grandpa's brother Greg and his wife Ruth were with us.

During the first scheduled meeting, Victoria saw a lot of angels and the Flaming Wild Horses. She also told us

Breakthrough was there but not all the way inside the building. He was just waiting.

PROPHETIC DRAWING

The next day we got there early to get good seats. Greg and Ruth were sitting in the middle beside Victoria with Sandi on the other side of her.

They witnessed Victoria looking rapidly around and up into the top of the church. Her eyes were darting all around. Then she would draw a picture.

She would look around some more and draw another picture. This went on for about 30 minutes with her looking and drawing.

She drew a series of five pictures. Those drawings are shown in the following pages. They included these sketches.

1. An eagle (Victoria said the eagles were in warfare)
2. A huge eagle flapping his wings making a tornado
3. An eagle plucking her feathers (molting)
4. A mother eagle looking down at a nest full of eggs
5. A dove

When Bob Jones got up he said he saw a whirlwind. He said that the eagles have fought for the harvest.

He said the eagles will molt and then dove feathers will grow back in. The young will be raised by doves. The harvest will be brought in by the doves.

JUST SOME ANGELS AND WILD HORSES

The next day, Friday, when I asked what was there… Victoria didn't see a lot. She said, "Not much, except a bunch of angels."

I persisted, "Are the wild horses here?"

Victoria just looked up from her coloring book and said, "Well, yeah. They're here."

As the service progressed, I was still seeking information and asked, "Look Victoria, the ministers are praying for the sick. Do they have healing angels with them?"

Victoria responded, "Yes."

Later as we were eating after the service was over, I asked her to tell me what she saw around each minister. She said, "Shawn Boltz haved an angel with him. Randy Demain haved an angel and Paul Keith haved an angel... but Bob Jones... he have a girl angel with him."

The next day Sandi took Victoria to the beach and we rode to church with Greg and Ruth.

Later, during the lunch break, the four of us went to eat together. As we got out of the car, I was prompted in my spirit to take a book into the restaurant. I put one in my purse and went on in.

When the food was put before us we bowed our head and Greg prayed a brief prayer and we said amen. We heard the word echoed from a table across from us. I looked over and a nice lady was sitting there smiling at us. I said, "Are you with the conference?"

She said, "Yes, I am."

I said, "I guess this is for you then." as I handed her the book, 6 Big Angels.

She looked at the title and gasped, and then almost screamed in surprise. She said, "I just heard about this from a lady today at the conference. You gave her a book at breakfast. I prayed that I would be able to find you and buy the book."

I told her it was a gift.

She told me she wanted it for her daughter who had a baby in heaven because of abortion and had just recently given birth to a lovely baby. She was sad now because she realized what she had done and how very much it had cost her.

I told her that the book would bring healing to her daughter. We pulled our tables together and had a lovely lunch.

Ruth Pennington, my sister in law volunteers at Solve,[8] a wonderful shelter in Bradenton, Florida for girls and women who choose not to abort. They either keep their baby or let it be adopted.

She had some interesting stories of success about the shelter and the brave women who provide care in two separate houses.

They have one house for young teenage girls and the other for mature women. They operate on contributions and need much more space than they have. They hope to build another shelter soon.

These homes and others over the US are valiantly providing a place of refuge for girls and women who have no other alternative, and no one to turn to.

These girls and women would possibly be having an abortion if not for shelters such as this.

---

[8] Manasota Solve, Inc.
1509 8th Ave. W.
Bradenton, FL 34205
www.manasotasolve.org

I SAW THAT!

We went back to the conference that night and I showed Victoria's little drawings to a minister. We had met him and his wife at the hotel the day before.

He said, "I saw an eagle last night. It was a big eagle, and then it was gone. I thought I was just seeing things.

I said, "You were. You were seeing into the supernatural."

Victoria drew these pictures before one of the night sessions at the Breakthrough Conference held at Titusville, Florida.

1. An eagle (Victoria said the eagles were in warfare)

2. A huge eagle flapping wings making a tornado or whirlwind

3. An eagle plucking her feathers (molting)

4. A mother eagle looking down at a nest full of eggs

5. A dove

CHAPTER 4

IT'S NOT MY TIME

RADIO AND TV

In late April 2006, we received a phone call from Messianic Vision[9]. This is the Ministry founded by Sid Roth, the host of the TV show, "It's Supernatural."

They said they had received our book, 6 Big Angels from a lady named Leila Baldwin.

UNIQUE MINISTRY

One of the reasons the people from Messianic Vision accepted the book so readily is because of Leila's unique ministry.

Leila Baldwin and her son Tim Baldwin who live in West Lebanon, New Hampshire have been ordering videos and books from Sid Roth for a long time and simply giving them away.

True to form, Leila bought a book from us and sent it to Sid Roth at Messianic Vision.

---

[9] Sid Roth
Messianic Vision
P. O. Box 1918
Brunswick, GA 31521
www.sidroth.org

ONE SEED, BIG HARVEST

In this single act of generosity, Leila and Tim are responsible for the distribution of thousands of our books all over the world.

Sid's programs are aired worldwide. We receive phone calls and emails from every continent on the earth.

Well, maybe not Antarctica... but we know it has gone to the Arctic. Many of the people of the Inuit Indian tribe have received and read the book.

FIRST SEED

Leila and Tim first received the book, 6 Big Angels from a friend of theirs who brought it from Florida.

As soon as they received it and started reading it, they called us and ordered three more books. Before we could get those books mailed they ordered more.

Tim is the first of many who called and said they saw a supernatural purple glow between the pages of the book.

They have been a constant blessing from that time. They have ordered many, many books and have given them all away. Leila and Tim have become very good and faithful friends.

They delight Victoria by sending her little tiny animals. She has received some very beautiful and delicate hand blown glass figures. One of her favorite things is a set of tiny wooden horses that have moving parts.

RADIO SHOW

Sid Roth's Messianic Vision wanted us to do a radio show first. They did the interview from our home. Sid tried several times to talk to Victoria, but was unsuccessful. At that time she was shy and had not yet been released by God.

They made an appointment for us to be in Charlotte the next month to film a segment for the TV show "It's Supernatural."

TV SHOW

We met Sid and all of the other participating ministries for dinner in the hotel restaurant. It was a private area with no other customers.

Sid sat beside Victoria to try to get acquainted with her and make friends. He wanted to persuade her to talk to him on camera the next day.

HORSE TALK

Sid had asked us on the phone before we went up there what Victoria likes. We told him she likes horses and that is what he talked about.

After some persuasion he convinced her to answer one question for him the next day. I'm not sure she really understood what he was asking.

IT'S NOT DIFFERENT FOR HER

As we were eating, a wave of supernatural presence swept over us. Sid slumped down in his seat and a sound came from him, "Hunhhh."

As we were sitting there, the presence of heaven was so heavy we almost had our heads in our plates. We could hardly hold our forks.

Sid asked Victoria if she felt that.

Victoria asked, "What?"

He asked, "Do you feel anything different?"

She looked around carefully and said, "No. Not really."

Sandi said to him, "Sid, she *lives* in that place… it's not different for her."

BIG ANGEL WITH A SHINY FACE

Then Jeff Jansen said, "My right hand is getting hot."

Sandi asked Victoria if she saw anything.

She told Sandi there was a very large angel standing behind Jeff and Sid. The angel had a hand on each of their heads and was praying for them.

Jeff asked her to describe the angel. She said his face was too shiny to see, but he had on a white robe with a gold belt.

Jeff told us that it is a healing angel. An angel that looks like that often shows up at his meetings.

MOVIN' FAST

Sid asked her if she saw anything else.

She told Sid, "I saw some things but they was moving *really* fast."

After we got to the room, she told us it was the "Four faces" that were moving around the table so fast. That is what she calls the living creatures. She said they were moving around really fast, making a lot of noise.

She saw God's throne just above the ceiling. I believe this is God's portable throne as spoken of in Ezekiel and Daniel.

HEAVENLY CARAVAN

Daniel 7:9-10
9 I watched till thrones were put in place,
And the Ancient of Days was seated;
His garment was white as snow,
And the hair of His head was like pure wool.

Could it be that He was just walking around before He got on His throne? Victoria told us one time that He could get into His throne. That was when she was not quite five years old, and was drawing the one that is on the back cover of 6 Big Angels. The door was so He could go inside.

FIERY WHEELS

His throne was a fiery flame,
Its wheels a burning fire;
10 A fiery stream issued
And came forth from before Him.
A thousand thousands ministered to Him;
Ten thousand times ten thousand stood before Him.

COURT IS IN SESSION

The court was seated,
And the books were opened.

Victoria has told us that she first saw God at the Baby Place. He was on His portable throne, carried by the "four faces with wheels and lots of eyes."

The throne she drew before she turned five years old *was* the portable throne.

We didn't understand everything she told us when she first came back from heaven.

As a matter of fact… we are still deficient in that area.

HEAVENS OPEN

Ezekiel 1:1,4 – 28
1 Now it came to pass in the thirtieth year, in the fourth month, on the fifth day of the month, as I was among the captives by the River Chebar, that the heavens were opened and I saw visions of God.

FIERY WHIRLWIND WITH RAGING FIRE

4 Then I looked, and behold, a whirlwind was coming out of the north, a great cloud with raging fire engulfing itself; and brightness was all around it and radiating out of its midst like the color of amber, out of the midst of the fire.

FOUR FACES, FOUR WINGS

5 Also from within it came the likeness of four living creatures. And this was their appearance: they had the likeness of a man.
6 Each one had four faces, and each one had four wings.

GLITTER FOOT

7 Their legs were straight, and the soles of their feet were like the soles of calves' feet. They sparkled like the color of burnished bronze.
8 The hands of a man were under their wings on their four sides; and each of the four had faces and wings.
9 Their wings touched one another. The creatures did not turn when they went, but each one went straight forward.

A MAN, A LION, AN OX AND AN EAGLE

10 As for the likeness of their faces, each had the face of a man; each of the four had the face of a lion on the right side, each of the four had the face of an ox on the left side, and each of the four had the face of an eagle.

11 Thus were their faces. Their wings stretched upward;
two wings of each one touched one another, and two
covered their bodies.
12 And each one went straight forward; they went
wherever the spirit wanted to go, and they did not turn
when they went.

RUNNING BACK AND FORTH

13 As for the likeness of the living creatures, their
appearance was like burning coals of fire, like the
appearance of torches going back and forth among the
living creatures. The fire was bright, and out of the fire
went lightning.
14 And the living creatures ran back and forth, in
appearance like a flash of lightning.

A WHEEL IN THE MIDDLE OF A WHEEL

15 Now as I looked at the living creatures, behold, a
wheel was on the earth beside each living creature with
its four faces.
16 The appearance of the wheels and their workings was
like the color of beryl, and all four had the same
likeness. The appearance of their workings was, as it
were, a wheel in the middle of a wheel.
17 When they moved, they went toward any one of four
directions; they did not turn aside when they went.

RIMS FULL OF EYES

18 As for their rims, they were so high they were
awesome; and their rims were full of eyes, all around
the four of them.
19 When the living creatures went, the wheels went
beside them; and when the living creatures were lifted
up from the earth, the wheels were lifted up.

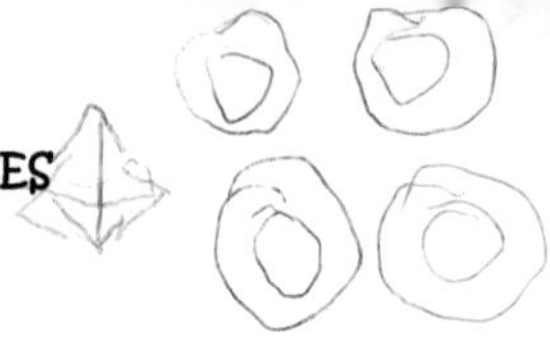

THERE HE GOES

20 Wherever the spirit wanted to go, they went, because
there the spirit went; and the wheels were lifted
together with them, for the spirit of the living creatures
was in the wheels.
21 When those went, these went; when those stood,
these stood; and when those were lifted up from the
earth, the wheels were lifted up together with them, for
the spirit of the living creatures was in the wheels.

AWESOME CRYSTAL FIRMAMENT

22 The likeness of the firmament above the heads of the
living creatures was like the color of an awesome crystal,
stretched out over their heads.
23 And under the firmament their wings spread out
straight, one toward another. Each one had two which
covered one side, and each one had two which covered
the other side of the body.
24 When they went, I heard the noise of their wings, like
the noise of many waters, like the voice of the Almighty,
a tumult like the noise of an army; and when they stood
still, they let down their wings.
25 A voice came from above the firmament that was
over their heads; whenever they stood, they let down
their wings.

SAPPHIRE THRONE

26 And above the firmament over their heads was the
likeness of a throne, in appearance like a sapphire
stone; on the likeness of the throne was a likeness with
the appearance of a man high above it.
27 Also from the appearance of His waist and upward I
saw, as it were, the color of amber with the appearance
of fire all around within it; and from the appearance of
His waist and downward I saw, as it were, the
appearance of fire with brightness all around.

A RAINBOW ON A CLOUDY DAY

28 Like the appearance of a rainbow in a cloud on a rainy day, so was the appearance of the brightness all around it. This was the appearance of the likeness of the glory of the LORD.

THRONE MOVERS

The creatures in Ezekiel face out and move Gods Throne. They move any direction the throne needs to go. They are very powerful and their chief purpose is to transport God's Portable Throne.

WORSHIP AROUND THE THRONE

Later when Jesus took her to the Throne Room, Victoria was startled by other creatures with one face each and lots of eyes. They were worshiping around God's throne in the Throne Room. Their only purpose is to worship God continually.

ONE FACE SIX WINGS

Rev 4:6-8
6 Before the throne there was a sea of glass, like crystal. And in the midst of the throne, and around the throne, were four living creatures full of eyes in front and in back.
7 The first living creature was like a lion, the second living creature like a calf, the third living creature had a face like a man, and the fourth living creature was like a flying eagle.
8 The four living creatures, each having six wings, were full of eyes around and within. And they do not rest day or night, saying:
"Holy, holy, holy,
Lord God Almighty,
Who was and is and is to come!"

She was frightened when she first saw them. For a long time she thought these guys were possibly demons. They looked different from the ones she had already seen at the "Baby Place." The ones at the baby place had rims with eyes. These creatures were full of eyes around and within.

They were around God's throne continually... worshipping Him. The other ones with four faces carry God around to different places to be seen by us.

Remember, God is omnipresent. Jesus Christ is God. Holy Spirit is God. They are not limited by location. They are God.

WIRED FOR SOUND

The next day all the ministries being filmed met to have lunch in the studio.

They prepared me with a microphone and positioned me on the set.

After they had me wired, Sid went over with the sound man and tried to get Victoria to let them place a microphone on her.

She said, "I am not going on TV."

Sid reminded her that she agreed to let him ask her one question.

She said she couldn't do that.

Sandi came over to the stage and I asked what was going on. She said they were going to see if she would let Jeff Jansen ask the question. Victoria really likes Jeff.

In fact, Jeff invited us to come to the Destiny Doors Conference in Nashville, Tennessee, because of this divine appointment at Sid Roth's filming session.

GOD SAID, 'IT'S NOT MY TIME'

Sandi and I briefly prayed for God's will to be done. If it wasn't her time, help her be strong. If it was OK to be on TV, help her not to be afraid.

Suddenly Sid walked up to the set and told me Victoria had the right answer.

He looked a little perplexed as he related their exchange.

Victoria looked him straight in the eye and told him, "God said, it's not time for me to be on TV yet."

Then Sid added, "You can't go any higher then that."

I had to agree... sometimes she will talk and sometimes she won't. I believe God lets her know when to just say no.

We filmed two segments that day.

After filming all day, the people that had participated went back to the hotel and ate dinner together.

When we finished dinner, Sid led us to an empty room to have a prayer meeting. It was a very sweet and powerful time of prayer. As we finished, we were all talking and enjoying fellowship together.

We had met Bill Weiss while we were in the studio, that day. Victoria really liked Bill and his wife, Annette.

GET THE PICTURE?

Bill is the author of "23 Minutes in Hell." In the book, he told about being locked in a cell with bars with a horrible, nasty demon.

Bill took out a picture. It was an artist's rendition of a demon that someone had seen in a death experience.

When Bill first saw the picture he recognized the demon as one he had encountered in hell. He asked Sandi if it would be all right to show it to Victoria.

Sandi said, “Sure, go ahead and let her see it.”

As he showed the picture to Victoria, he said, “Victoria, have you ever seen this demon?”

She glanced at the picture and answered emphatically, “Oh yeah! That’s Howlschmoo! He howls a lot! He’s a really good howler!”

Then she looked more closely at the picture, a puzzled look on her face and said, “Only ’cept… Howlschmoo’s face…? It’s not quite that long... and his ear... it’s not that low...” she pointed her finger at a particular spot on the picture and said, “It’s right here.”

Bill was surprised that she noticed such detail and said, “You are exactly right, Victoria. When I scanned it into my computer, it became elongated and distorted.”

PEW PESTS

Victoria has seen demons in many places since she went down to the bad place. One of the most surprising things is that she sees demons in many churches that she visits. They are usually sitting on or beside the people in the pews.

POTTY PATROL

She said they all look very much alike. Their job is to “pee pee, poo poo and throw up” on all the church goers.

REVELATIONS OF HELL

After we filmed our segments of “It’s Supernatural”, Victoria and I were talking about the experience and the people we met there. She mentioned Bill Wiese and said how much she loved him and Annette.

She said, "He went down to the bad place, too. He saw a lot of demons, too. He was even locked in with some of them."

She knew this because she heard part of his TV interview.

PRIVATE HELL

Then unexpectedly she said, "I know what he said was true. I saw caves with bars on them... people were locked in there... They were naked... and terrible demons were in there with them."

She continued, "I saw a naked man in a dark nasty cave with bars on it... and I saw a horrible looking smelly demon in there with him. That demon had really, really, **really** *LONG,* TERRIBLE *AWFUL* fingernails, that lookeded like *CLAWS."*

Then to my dismay she said, "You know that thing that hangs down in the front of a man's privates?"

Once again she shocked me and even though I was stunned, I had to admit, "Yes, Honey, I know."

She went on with the gruesome narrative, "That nasty smelly demon reached out his hand with those awful jaggedy dirty claws and actually grabbed that thing and ripped it right off... just ripped it off with his claws.

"Then he slashed off one of that man's butt cheeks with his fingernails... and you know what that demon did with his butt cheek after he ripped it off? He ate it! Then he slashed off the other butt cheek with his fingernails and ate it!

"After the demon tore off the man's butt and privates, you know what happened? They just grew back and the demon ripped them off over and over again."

These horrible and explicit revelations were almost more than I could bear.

I DON'T KNOW HOW TO HANDLE THAT

She was only five and a half years old when she went to the bad place. I don't know how she was able to handle the things she saw and experienced.

She was so little when she told us about the people she saw in the bad place and in the water... *FIREwater* and they stayed there a hundred years and you never die... we could hardly bear to hear it. She had said it so clearly at the time, "They was so skinny and bald headed and I just don't know how to handle that."

She had already revealed much that happened on that trip, but here she was after such a long time, confiding more about that terrible trip to the bad place. That journey through Hades happened more than two years before, when she swam down under the float in our pool and disappeared.

She *did* have Jesus with her on that trip and she said it so clearly when she finally told us about it, ***"Jesus is the King. 'Cause He could even protect a wee little girl like me."***

CHAPTER 5

TODAY I'M NOT GOING TO LOOK UP OR DOWN

Rachael, one of our granddaughters, had just given birth to a precious baby girl and we were on the way to West Palm Beach to see our new great grandbaby.

We had made a bed in the middle seat so Victoria could either play or lay down.

As we turned onto Lumsden Road and headed East, Victoria stretched out on the bed on her stomach and looked out the left window right behind Grandpa's head.

She said, "Majo, I'm going to look out the window on this side for horses and cows and you look out that side. If you see any horses or cows, tell me and I will look out that side."

I agreed and turned my head and started searching the passing scenery for animals.

Then she added grimly, "Today, I'm not looking up *or* down."

I sat speechless in the passenger seat of the old Suburban. I couldn't believe what I had just heard, and what it implied. I turned and looked at Grandpa. He looked surprised, too.

Previously she had told Sandi she could see Jesus and God when she looks up.

When her mommy asked her how she deals with that as she goes out to play with other kids... she had said, "I just don't look up."

However, she had never mentioned anything happening when she looked down.

I carefully kept my voice normal as I asked Victoria to explain.

IT'S THE PITS

I said quietly, "Victoria, I know that when you look up you often see into heaven and can even see God, but what do you see when you look down?"

She quickly scooted over to my side of the car and pointed down toward the ditch on the side of the road.

In an agitated voice she said, "Well, you tell me what *you* see when *you* look down there."

I tentatively guessed, "Demons?"

She said, "Yes... and what else do you see?"

She looked at me intently as I stretched around to see her face. I knew she saw more... and not only that... she thought it was normal, and that I could see them, too.

I ventured another guess, "You can see down into the pit?"

"Well, Yeah!" She answered as though I should already know that.

I knew she had been to the "bad place" when she was only five and a half years old. I thought it was a one-time thing. Jesus had taken her there to show her His power and might. That she didn't have to be afraid of demons because His Name is all powerful.

I knew she could see demons and pray against them if they got too close.

Sandi had taught her to pray, In the name of Jesus Christ, you have to go.

HANDBOOK FOR GRANDPARENTS

We should be accustomed to this by now, but once again, I was caught off guard.

She had just revealed another aspect of her ability to see into the spirit realm and it was terrible to contemplate.

I was torn. One prophet had told me that she doesn't *have* to see the demons. We could pray and prevent that and she would only see the angels.

I almost started trying to bind and rebuke the evil spirits.

Then I hesitated, as I thought… *"Maybe this is another thing God wants to use for her instruction. Maybe He is preparing her for a destiny that we can't even imagine."*

There isn't a handbook on how to raise a child seer.

I looked at Grandpa again and he just shrugged an "I don't know," at me. We have become pretty good at silent signals.

I just silently began to pray for God's will to be done and for Jesus to give her the strength to endure.

STRENGTH TO ENDURE

> TIMOTHY 2:1-3; 11-12
> 1 You therefore, my son, be strong in the grace that is in Christ Jesus.

2 And the things that you have heard from me among many witnesses, commit these to faithful men who will be able to teach others also.

ENDURE HARDSHIP

3 You therefore must endure hardship as a good soldier of Jesus Christ.

IF WE DIE, WE LIVE

11 This is a faithful saying:
For if we died with Him,
We shall also live with Him.

IF WE ENDURE, WE REIGN

12 If we endure,
We shall also reign with Him.

I prayed for the Holy Spirit to lead us through this. I felt that God was teaching her something. I just prayed for His will to be done and to give her the strength and understanding to go through this experience with valor.

She didn't mention it again and we stayed busy looking out the windows for farm animals.

A little over an hour later, we stopped at Yee Haw Junction and went into the old historic cafe to get a soda.

She found some little "banty" chickens with tiny little baby chicks and played with them for a while. She fed them some ground corn made available by the cafe.

At this time, she was out on the ground, squatting down, trying to coax the babies closer to her.

I observed her carefully and she didn't seem to be alarmed about being out of the car and on the ground. Whatever she had seen in Brandon apparently was *not* going on at Yee Haw Junction.

We drove on to West Palm Beach to see saw Rachael's precious new baby. As Victoria carefully held Rachael's baby, I could just picture her cuddling the tiny babies in heaven.

She met with Tara, another one of our granddaughters who is doing the art work for the first children's book. She took notes as Victoria described the 6 Big Angels in detail.

The children's book is going to have wonderful pictures of the beautiful angels that caught Victoria when she was only four and a half years old.

All of this happened in a single day.

While we watched her holding the wonder of a new born baby in her arms, it was difficult to imagine what she had experienced earlier that very day.

She went from looking into the pits of the bad place to describing the 6 big, beautiful angels that caught her three years earlier and zoom, "tooked" her to heaven.

God's grace is sufficient.

CHAPTER 6

LITTLE BABY GOAT

LEILA AND TIM'S CHURCH

We had only planned to go to New Hampshire to visit Leila Baldwin and her son Tim. Leila is the lady we mentioned earlier who sent a copy of the book 6 Big Angels to Sid Roth.

Leila told her pastor, Dee Copley, we were coming. Dee asked us to speak in the Sunday night service at their church, the White Horse Café[10] in Vermont.

The message we delivered was about the knowledge of the Glory of God. We related how God had used a little girl to bring back the knowledge of the glory of God.

> Habakkuk 2: 3, 11, 14
> 3 For the vision is yet for an appointed time;
> But at the end it will speak, and it will not lie.
> Though it tarries, wait for it;
> Because it will surely come,
> It will not tarry.

---

10 Pastor Dee Copley
Revival Connections
P O Box 516, 1581 Rt. 14,
Hartford VT 05047-0516
phone: 802-295-5248

> 11 For the stone will cry out from the wall,
> And the beam from the timbers will answer it.
>
> 14 For the earth will be filled
> With the knowledge of the glory of the LORD,
> As the waters cover the sea.

Our job was made easy. Leila and Tim had given almost every person in this church a copy of the book. We were speaking to an audience that had already read the book and believed it.

A SPLIT SECOND

After Sandi prayed and brought us into a powerful anointing from the Holy Spirit, Grandpa explained about Victoria's fall.

He thought he should always tell the beginning just in case there could possibly be a single person there who had not read the book.

I explained that much of what you read in the book took just a few seconds to happen as Victoria fell off the slide.

Luke tells about something that happened in the spirit realm that took only a brief moment. The devil showed Jesus all the kingdoms of the world in a moment of time. A single moment.

> Luke 4:5
> 5 Then the devil, taking Him up on a high mountain, showed Him all the kingdoms of the world in a moment of time.

NEW DETAILS OF THE GLORY

We made this trip right after we were at Sid Roth's and before we went to Nashville, Tennessee. We had no idea how much God was beginning to show Victoria, because she was very private about it.

Our approach was still that we were just a couple of grandparents telling about our granddaughter's experiences and the Knowledge of the Glory.

At this point she had not told us about the Healing Angel that was already with us.

SANCTIFY MY IMAGINATION

As I started to speak, I knew I had to tell them about the children's book because they had already read Six Big Angels. I knew I had to give them new details and new experiences that they hadn't already read about.

I told them that their imagination is a God given tool for His use. Then we prayed for Him to sanctify their mind and imagination so they could see heaven as we described it. I asked them to close their eyes. Whatever they saw on that little screen just in front of their eyes they could know it was from God.

Then I started telling about the children's book and many of the details about heaven that Victoria has revealed as she matured. People had their eyes closed and slid down in their chairs to relax and be ready to see into the heavenlies.

NOTES FROM THE CHILDRENS BOOK

The following is a narrative of Victoria's original trip to heaven when she fell from the swimming pool sliding board in 2003.

It has many additional details that she has revealed to us over time. Most of this will be in the children's book. That is why we simply tell about the babies that Jesus heals and makes whole, with no mention of the fact that most of them are there as the result of abortion.

If you have read 6 Big Angels some of this will sound familiar. However, we feel that the new details will be a blessing to you. We hope those of you who have not read the first book, will do so.

TRIP OF A LIFETIME

When Victoria fell off the slide in 2003, six big angels caught her and took her to Heaven.

She described the Angels in the following way; one have red hair, one have light orange hair, one have golden hair, one have bright shiny hair (Flames), one have shine bright, silvery hair, and one have light purple hair that is kind of blue.

The one that had flames on him held her upper body and arm on one side. She told us that as he held her hand and arm, little flames would run up her arm and hand because he had flames all over him.

She said it "lookeded like fire... but it didn't burn."

SHINE LIKE A LIGHTBULB

When these beautiful angels caught Victoria in their very large, warm hands, they were shining brightly. Victoria said they made her shine like a light bulb.

As they lifted her away from the sliding board and started to zoom up toward the sky, they passed an airplane going sideways and they were going straight up.

They passed all the clouds and beautiful blue sky. The Angels told her to look back to see the earth. At first it was like a big round horizon and then as they zoomed upward it became like a big ball and then it got smaller and smaller and looked like a little ball.

THINK ABOUT IT

The big angels laughed and sang songs so she would not

be afraid. They sang songs in a different language but Victoria could understand them. She knew every word! She was very surprised.

They could even tell her things without speaking. They would think it, and then she would know what they said.

As these beautiful angels started through the second heaven with Victoria, terrible demons started rushing at her.

NICE TRY, GUYS

Beautiful “Heaven Horses” flew to her rescue.

The 6 big angels put her on the back of a beautiful horse as they turned to fight the demons.

Many big angels that looked like fighters came to help them.

These angels had on armor and fought with swords and lances. Their armor was golden and they carried huge golden shields.

They were riding on big horses. They kept the demons away from Victoria as they sped on up past the second heaven.

As Victoria and the horses approached the golden stairs her six big angels swooped back in and took her in their hands again and carried her on up the stairs.

OPEN! OPEN!

As they traveled up the golden stairs, there was a little girl Angel who flew alongside her and tickled her and they laughed and laughed.

The six big angels stood her on her feet in front of a beautiful golden gate. The little angel girl came and put her arm around Victoria to keep her from falling. Victoria was swaying with a little dizziness.

THE LAUGH'S ON YOU

Then the little girl Angel ran over and tickled the gate with her feather. The Big Beautiful Gate laughed, and swung open.

The little Angel girl looked at Victoria and they both laughed. The six big angels were laughing. The horses were laughing and the gate was still laughing, too.

GREEN, GREEN GRASS OF HOME

Victoria stepped inside the gate. At first she thought she was stepping on a green rug it was so perfect. When she looked closer she was surprised to see lovely living green grass under her feet.

She lifted her foot; the grass sprang back up and seemed to say, "Hello! Hello! Hello, Victoria!"

Victoria was a little embarrassed because she had never talked to grass before, so she leaned over and whispered, *"Hello grass."*

Victoria took another step. She realized she was still stepping on the grass and quickly lifted her foot. The grass sprang back up, laughing.

Victoria quickly stepped onto a walkway. She thought this walkway was made of concrete. Then she looked again, and saw that it was gold! Gold concrete!

HEAVENLY CHOIR

She took a few steps and saw on each side of the golden path, lots and lots of beautiful flowers of every color.

As Victoria told me later, "I saw lots and lots of beautiful flowers. They smelled so good I was sniffing them... sniff, sniff. They smelled like roseberries. I picked a berry off one of them and ate it. It was very good."

She looked again, and stepped closer. The beautiful flowers had faces. They reached toward her with their leafy hands. They offered her some roseberries from their little green leaf hands. They were reaching out and offering them to her. She ate some more.

The flower faces were nodding at her and then they started singing. They sang this beautiful song to Victoria.

Victoria you are welcome here
We want to play with you
Will you please sit down with us
We'll make you smell good too

The flower faces said, "Sit down, Victoria, sit down! Sit down, Victoria!"

Victoria carefully sat down on the flowers. She did not want to mash them because they had faces. But the flowers kept saying, "Sit *down*, Victoria."

Victoria relaxed and sat there looking at the beautiful heaven flowers. They smelled so good.

Then the flowers said, "Lay down, Victoria, lay down."

As Victoria reluctantly lay down, the flowers started tickling her with their little petals. Then they started to sing, "Roll over, roll over, roll over!"

The beautiful heaven flowers started laughing. They tickled Victoria as she rolled over and over.

Victoria was laughing, the flowers were laughing and

Victoria's six big angels were laughing, too.

As Victoria rolled over, the perfume from the flowers covered her and she began to smell like heaven. The pollen from the flowers began to cover Victoria and it was golden glitter. She began to look shiny like heaven. She was clothed in the Glory of Heaven and drenched in the fragrance of heaven.

> 2 Cor 2:14-15
> 14 Now thanks be to God who always leads us in triumph in Christ, and through us diffuses the fragrance of His knowledge in every place.
> 15 For we are to God the fragrance of Christ among those who are being saved and among those who are perishing.

DO YOU WANT TO SEE JESUS

A beautiful lady Angel was coming down the path to meet her. She came up to Victoria and said, "Is your name Victoria?"

Victoria stood up and stepped back onto the golden concrete pathway and answered, "Yes, my name is Victoria."

The beautiful angel lady said, "Do you want to see Jesus?"

Victoria quickly answered, "Yes, I really *do* want to see Jesus."

The angel lady said, "Do you want to play with some babies?"

Victoria said, "Yes!"

TRAMPOLINE OF HEAVEN

She waved goodbye to her 6 Big Angels and started up the

path with the angel. As she walked, she noticed that her steps were springy. Each time she put her foot on the golden walkway she would bounce a little bit. She felt very light.

She decided to try a jump. When she did, she bounced very high. She bounced again, only higher this time. Soon she was bouncing almost up to the sky.

Her angel lady was bouncing just as high as Victoria was. Victoria felt as though she could fly.

DESTINATION, HEAVENLY NURSERY

Victoria looked ahead and saw all kinds of trees and bushes and flowers. She saw a huge building shining in the distance. It was shaped like a dome.

The angel told her that the dome was the Baby Place.

Even though the dome looked far away in the distance, suddenly Victoria and the lady Angel were there.

They entered the baby place and Victoria saw a wonderful room that was big and round with lots of soft white tables all the way around. The tables looked as soft as clouds.

HEAVEN HAS ITS UPS AND DOWNS

There was a spiral rainbow going up the center of this beautiful room all the way to the ceiling that was high above them.

There was a beautiful elevator of light that went up and down the rainbow. She saw people in beautiful robes riding up and others riding down this elevator of light.

As the elevator came down the rainbow, people would get off. Then other people would step onto the elevator and ride up the rainbow to the top of the dome. The elevator went through the roof of the dome.

TIME FOR RESTORATION

Victoria looked at the tables that encircled the room and saw beautiful angels holding tiny little babies. Some of the babies were so tiny you couldn't see them. You could only see a light held gently in the hands of the angel.

Some angels held tiny babies and others held larger babies. Some appeared to be as big as a newborn baby.

As Jesus walked down the rows of tables, the Angels gently placed their precious baby in front of Him. Jesus would touch them and make them whole. Every organ in their body was made new and whole.

As He healed them, He gave them beautiful faces, strong arms and legs and a brain that already knew a lot of things.

Victoria noticed that they could speak instantly as though they were bigger, but they were tiny. She was puzzled. She had never seen a tiny baby that could talk. The tiny babies thanked Jesus for healing them.

The angels picked each tiny baby up and placed it in a beautiful little baby bed that just fit each tiny baby.

Victoria saw many, many babies. They were in front of her, and behind her, on the left of her and to the right of her. She thought there must be at least sixty.

Recently, as I read this account to Victoria, she said, "There were probably millions of babies there that day."

All the babies smiled at Jesus and thanked him for the love and healing He brought to them.

LEARNING THE TRUTH

Then an expanse of the ceiling rolled open and they saw something that was almost like a movie. Victoria thought it *was* a movie but they came out and were real. They saw this very quickly, in a moment of time.

LOST WORLD

Jesus showed these tiny babies the world, and how men were lost without a Savior. He showed them that he alone could save the world. He was the only sacrifice that was worthy to pay for the sins of man. He was their only hope.

They saw the complete life of Jesus.

They saw when Gabriel came to Mary and she was honored above all women as he told her that she was chosen to give birth to the Son of God.

Victoria and the babies watched as Mary tried to tell Joseph, the man she was going to marry. Then they watched as Gabriel came to him and told him, “Do not fear to take Mary as your wife.”

FIRST PRAISE WORSHIP SERVICE

They watched as Mary gave birth to Jesus in Bethlehem of Judea. They watched as she placed him in the manger and the shepherds came to worship him.

The babies learned to worship him from the shepherds. They were shouting and praising God for the birth of the Messiah, the Savior of the world.

Some of the babies knelt down beside their little tiny bed to worship Jesus. Some tiny babies lifted their hands in praise.

Victoria and the babies saw Jesus as he grew up. They

saw all of the events of his life leading up to his ministry. They watched as He helped his earthly father, Joseph build chairs, tables, and other things. They were carpenters.

They watched as Jesus was baptized by John in the Jordan River and the Holy Spirit descended as a Dove.

They saw as Jesus and the disciples went around preaching and doing good. They learned all about the teachings of Jesus and the miracles of Jesus.

They saw that many people loved Jesus and accepted his teachings. They saw the priests of the temple as they turned on Jesus and wanted to kill him.

They watched in horror as Jesus was dragged before the officials and then they couldn't believe their eyes when he was beaten. Victoria and all the babies were crying.

Their eyes got bigger when they watched as Jesus laid his body down and stretched out his hands. Then the soldiers put the big spikes to His flesh, raised the hammer, and nailed Him to the cross. Their mouths were open with horror as the spikes pierced His hands and feet and the blood began to well up and drip off.

As the cross was lifted up by the soldiers and dropped down into the hole with a thud, they moaned with grief. They saw that it ripped his hands and feet and caused them to bleed even more than they already were.

The babies could not believe it when Jesus died. They watched as the sky grew dark and the earth quaked.

Later, as the soldiers went around breaking the legs of the two thieves, the babies were relieved that Jesus was already dead. They did not break his bones.

The babies watched as a spear was thrust into His side and blood and water poured forth.

They were beyond words and tears poured down their faces as He was sealed inside the tomb.

JESUS IS ALIVE

Then the darkness totally disappeared as light burst from the tomb.

They cheered with joy as they saw Him come out. The babies and Victoria were tumbling and turning somersaults and shouting, “He's alive! Jesus is alive!”

As they watched this panorama of wonder and Glory, it was as if they saw it all at one time. As it ended, Jesus, Victoria and the babies were laughing and jumping around.

PARTY TIME

Jesus looked at a special Angel and nodded. The Special Angel smiled and winked at some Special Food Angels and some of the Redeemed Saints who danced in with trays of wonderful fruit.

The babies and Victoria ate the fruit and loved it. As they ate, the juice dripped down their chins and arms. Jesus touched them and the juice went into His body.

The Angels and Redeemed Saints brought cups of milk and wonderful nectar and the Water of Life. They ate and drank all they wanted. It was like a big party.

I continued to tell the people in Vermont about the wonders of the baby place. Many looked as if they were asleep, but I knew they were drinking in the wonders of heaven and seeing it in their own mind and imagination.

ALL ABOARD!

Then Victoria and some of the babies that were close to her went into the elevator of light and rode up through the roof.

Their angels went with them. As they stepped out onto the roof... the rainbow turned into hundreds of rainbows going in different directions.

Victoria and her group stepped into a "rainbow light room" with their angels and "ZOOP!" they were at another place that had wonderful rooms for the babies.

FIRST CLASS ACCOMMODATIONS

Amazingly, their little beds were already there, all perfect and lovely, their own beds from the Baby Place. There was one for each baby. It was here Victoria met Alcie... Little Victoria... Majolynn... and the Garbage Baby. They are the ones that Jesus let her name.

Their room was very beautiful with flowers growing on the walls and rainbows in front of the flowers. The ceiling was like a real sky with stars.

ZOO PARADE

Later, a wonderful kangaroo angel sang to them and let the babies get into her pouch. This comforted the babies as some of them pretended it was their mommy's tummy. The kangaroo jumped around so funny they had to laugh.

The precious baby that Victoria gave her own name to, "Little Victoria" snuggled down into the sweet smelling pouch and thought about how much she loved her mommy and she missed her, too.

But, she didn't have time to feel bad... Victoria and the other babies were pulling her out of the kangaroo pouch. They wanted to explore.

The babies went out into the yard that was a park with beautiful flowers and fruit trees. They rode on little deer and horses and played with rabbits, lions and birds.

Every animal in every color was in this park. They could sing, talk to the children and fly. They also smelled very nice. And everybody, animals and kids could laugh!

SNOW BOUND

They saw a lovely light purple mountain with snow on it. A beautiful rainbow reached down to the top of the mountain. Victoria wanted to go up the mountain to see the snow.

They "float flied" instantly over to the mountain and tumbled into the snow. She was surprised to find the snow was not cold. It was just beautiful and fun.

RAIN OR SHINE

Then they went up to the rainbow and "dived up" into it. They "swim flied" in the swift current of the rainbow.

The rainbow took them up to a beautiful cloud. They jumped out of the rainbow onto the cloud and started bouncing up and down.

Victoria told me when she was only seven years old, "It is really cool up there. It is raining glory up in the cloud."

I said, "Do you mean raining glory... like the gold dust? Like the glory dust?"

She said, "Yes, it is raining glory in the cloud, and lots of toys up there."

Tiny beautiful animals of every size were bouncing on the clouds too. They were every color you could imagine. The tiny babies and the teeny animals played and bounced together.

OVER THE RAINBOW

Later Victoria, the babies and the little animals jumped into the swift rainbow current again. They slid down the other side and landed in a pile of gold dust.

Victoria became even more covered with golden glitter than she was when the flowers covered her with pollen. She fit right in with the Glory Crowd of Heaven.

The babies picked up the teddy bears or any other little animal they wanted to play with. The tiny animal was exactly the right size for their tiny little hand to hold.

When each baby kissed its little tiny animal, the angel animal turned another color and started singing. This was a great surprise! The angel animals could change to any color the babies wanted.

UP A CREEK WITH A PADDLE

Then they clamored into a little canoe that was right beside the river of life, and they floated down to the baby place. Their tiny angel animals were singing, so the children and Victoria joined in. They were singing, laughing, and splashing their hands in the River of Life.

I decided to tell this hungry crowd a couple more sweet little things that Victoria had shared with us about other trips to heaven.

NEW CUSTOMERS

Another time when Victoria went to heaven, she saw a big… big… big… table. She explained, "It was a beautiful table that have carving on it and beautiful legs and it have a big… big… big… big cake on it." She said the cake was delicious because it was chocolate. "It have a big, big bowl of ice cream beside it."

It was a special chocolate cake for the Redeemed ones that had just arrived. It was for the "new customers."

MILK AND HONEY

As Victoria grew and matured, she could tell us more about the wonders of heaven.

When she was only six and a half, she told Mommy that there are two rivers side by side in heaven with just a little land between them. One is milk and the other is honey.

When Sandi told me about the milk and honey, I decided to try to find out more details about this episode.

I called Victoria in and asked her if I could ask her one question.

She said, cheerfully, “Yes, I’ll answer one question for you.”

I said, “Your mom told me that you saw two rivers side by side in heaven, one with milk and one with honey...

She nodded and agreed that she had seen them in heaven.

I continued, “So as the milk and honey was flowing along, what was under it... what was on the river banks?”

GOLDEN RIVER BANKS

Using her hands to indicate a scooped out place or riverbed she said, “It have like gold under it and up the sides.”

Of course, I couldn’t stop with just one question. So pushing a little bit I asked, “Were these big rivers or just smaller rivers.”

She said, “Just kinda like smaller rivers.”

I said, “Not big like the river of life?”

She said, “No, not big like that.”

Then I asked if there was anything else on the banks or on the gold and she said, "No, just the gold."

I asked her if people had to dip into it with something. She replied, "Yes, something like a cup."

Then I said, "You told us that the river of life came up in many beautiful fountains all over heaven..." She nodded as I continued, "By chance does the milk and honey have a fountain?"

She was feeling pushed and said quietly, "I don't know... that is enough."

She did add a little later that the river of life flows over a bed of something like very shiny sand that looks like tiny pearls with jewels and diamonds. Flowers and trees grow all along the banks.

CHOCOLATE, CHOCOLATE

As so often happens, when we ask about one thing it reminds her of something else.

Talking about the milk and honey rivers did just that.

She told her mommy later that night that she and the babies went to a very special river that flows in the baby place. It is a chocolate river and has golden riverbanks, too.

It has wonderful trees growing along the sides of it and the leaves are very good.

She said you just pick a leaf off of the tree and dip it into the flowing chocolate.

There are vanilla leaves, mint leaves, strawberry leaves and very tasty caramel leaves.

Some of the leaves are chocolate and the babies like those best of all. They dip the chocolate leaves into the chocolate river and it makes them very smart and very happy. It also gives them lots of energy. Victoria tried dipping some chocolate leaves into the chocolate river. She said, “It is the best thing I have ever tasted in my whole life.”

> Rev 22:2
> 2 ...The leaves of the tree were for the healing of the nations.

Everybody knows... if you want children to like something... you put chocolate on it.

ON A DIET

She referred to the chocolate river and the giant ice cream bowl several times. She mentioned it especially when she had to be careful and not eat much sugar and chocolate here on the earth.

She asked Mommy one day, “Why I can eat as much chocolate in heaven as I want and it doesn’t make me fat?”

Sandi told her she didn’t know how that happened and then added dryly, “You should enjoy it while you are in heaven because you certainly can’t have a lot of it here.”

IMPARTATION

As I finished sharing the precious baby place experiences with this receptive New England crowd, there was a wonderful presence of the Holy Spirit. We should have prayed a prayer of impartation over this hungry crowd. But, we didn’t know about that then. We didn’t realize that it was possible. But God did.

After we finished speaking, we turned the service over to Kevin Ford of SoZo Ministries. Kevin and his wife Cynthia have a unique healing ministry and they enjoy a heavy anointing of the glory.

Soon we were having such a happy time together, the Fords and us, laying hands on everybody that wanted prayer. We were taking our first steps into learning about impartation that night.

BABY GOAT

We stayed another day and enjoyed the beauty of the countryside. The church is located on a large piece of property that is somewhat rural and is adjacent to some agricultural fields. There were open areas with animals, including some goats.

On Monday morning, Sandi and Victoria went out to see the goats. There were mother goats and baby goats and Victoria was delighted to watch them. The mother goats led the baby goats up the mountain and left a little black baby goat at the bottom.

This little black baby goat was sick. His eyes were infected and he really looked thin. As he lay there watching as the rest of the goats went further away, he started crying and bleating. He struggled, trying to get to his feet. He tried to get up several times but finally subsided in weakness.

HEALING ANGEL

Victoria said, “Mommy, can we pray for that baby goat?”

Sandy said, “Of course we can. Sandi and Victoria bowed their heads and prayed.

When they finished praying, Victoria said, “Mommy, when you prayed for that baby goat, the Healing Angel came and picked him up and healed him and then put him back down.”

The baby goat soon got to his feet and scampered up the mountain to the mothers and babies. Victoria was very happy!

Sandi asked Victoria if the healing angel is the one we saw at Sid Roth and she said yes it is the same one. That is the first time we realized that a healing angel travels with us.

Dee called a few days later and told us that the entire congregation had been lifted to a new level. Some were seeing angels and she had been having dreams and visions about heaven like she never had before.

WASHINGTON, DC

When we left Vermont, we headed for a visit with our home church, Abundant Love Christian Fellowship, located in Washington, DC.

We arrived in DC on Wednesday in time for the service that night. They always let us tell about the latest Victoria episode.

After I finished speaking and went to sit down. I was sitting beside a lady who said to me, "I hear the sound of eternity in your voice. What is that? I want it."

I could only think of one thing to say. I quoted the scripture in Habakkuk 2:14. *"And the earth will be filled with the knowledge of the glory of the Lord, as the waters cover the sea."*

She repeated again, "But, I hear the sound of eternity in your voice. What is that? I *want* that."

Again, I said, *"And the earth will be filled with the* ***knowledge*** *of the glory of the Lord as the waters cover the sea."*

She said, "I think I get it. I think I get it!"

I was not even aware at that time, the reason I quoted that Scripture. I have thought of it many times, trying to figure out what she heard in my voice, and why the Lord gave me that scripture.

I believe, because we know about the secrets of heaven, as told to us by Victoria, that we are *aware* of the ***knowledge*** of the glory of the Lord.

It is the knowledge of heaven and the glory of the Lord that makes the difference.

Our thoughts are always in that place of glory... turning it over in our minds... about the last one she told us about... the one we don't *quite* understand yet.

THE UPPER ROOM

We spent the night with our pastors, Tom and Sue Breuner in Washington, DC in what they call the Upper Room. We, like so many others, have seen angels in that room.

We were loading the suburban to go down to Ashland, Virginia to the CPT campground when I received a phone call from that same lady. She wanted to talk about the glory of God. She hoped to hear again, the sound of eternity.

I started telling her about the children's book and the details that Victoria has told us for that book. As I started telling her about the laughing gate and the flowers with faces and the grass that said hello Victoria, she started laughing. I started laughing, too.

As I was telling her about Victoria jumping high on the golden pathway, she was laughing so hard she fell out of bed.

I was trying to hold on to the wall, but I fell on the floor anyway. I couldn't stop laughing and neither could she.

Finally, I realized I couldn't talk anymore, and I just gasped out that I was going to hang up the phone.

It was quite a while before I could stand up. Grandpa finished loading the Suburban. I had Victoria on one side and Grandpa on the other helping me walk out to the car and get in.

As we drove through Washington, Victoria started telling me what she saw while I was laughing.

She said Mikey was in there on a big horse watching me…

That sobered me up pretty quickly! I ask her what *he* was doing.

She answered, “Mikey was laughing.” Then she added, “The horse was laughing too.”

I asked Grandpa, “What is Mikey doing in Washington, DC. anyway! He’s supposed to be watching over Israel!”

Grandpa said, “Is it possible that Mikey is here in DC because of the current crisis in Israel? It *is* lunch time, maybe Mikey is just taking a lunch break to come over here and mess with you.”

CHAPTER 7

THE BEGINNING OF TIME

It was after she went to the bad place in June 2004 that Victoria first told me about The Teenage Boy. She told me to write it down in a little book that she handed me. She said, "Write this down, I am only going to tell you once."

I wrote it down and recorded it with a little tape recorder in my pocket.

In the first book, 6 Big Angels, I grouped The Teenage Boy with the babies and children she met on her first trip when she fell from the slide.

It was eight months later when she admitted that she had been to the bad place. It took almost two years for me to understand about *when* she met The Teenage Boy.

BROKEN HORN

Immediately after she left the bad place, Jesus took her on up to the Baby Place. She saw her friends, Alcie, Majo Lynn, Garbage Baby and Little Victoria.

As she was leaving the baby girls section of the Baby Place, she heard some strange and very beautiful music. It was coming from the boy's section of the "Children's Place" that she had just decided to explore.

She walked along until she found where the music was

coming from. She looked into a window and saw a teenage boy writing a song. Jesus Christ was helping him.

We related that account in the first book, 6 Big Angels.

They invited her in and when she came into the room, the very old instrument The Teenage Boy was holding had broken. Jesus and The Teenage Boy asked her to help them fix it.

She had picked up some of the gold glory dust and it was on her hand. When they asked her to fix the old instrument, without any question she stepped forward to obey.

As she reached out to touch the old instrument, her hand was shining and glittering with the golden substance. She touched the instrument and “ZOOP!” it went back together and “was healed.”

HOW DID HE DO THAT?

After the healing of the old instrument, Jesus Christ came outside with Victoria. That is when she saw the other children she had become acquainted with on her first trip.

Victoria, with the eight boys and eight girls danced in a circle along with the babies. They sang songs to Jesus the King as The Teenage Boy played beautiful music.

When she was only seven, we were talking about the day she fixed the old instrument. I asked her what instrument The Teenage Boy was playing at the window for her and the babies to dance.

She said he was playing the old instrument and a violin at the same time. It was almost as though he had another hand but he didn't.

She murmured with a puzzled little frown, "I just couldn't figure how he was doing it all at one time."

FREQUENT VISITOR

The Teenage Boy is very important to Victoria. He and Little Victoria often come to see her.

Little Victoria is the granddaughter of friends of ours. The early account of this little girl is in our first book 6 Big Angels. We will give an update about her and her mommy in another chapter.

LUCIFER'S ROBE

When Victoria was seven she told me some more about The Teenage Boy. I was sitting at the computer working on the manuscript for "Big Angels and Flaming Wild Horses" when she came to me.

She said. "The Teenage Boy... His robe is very beautiful. It is almost as beautiful as the robe that Lucifer wore when he still loved God."

I spun around and looked at her standing quietly beside me.

I was stunned! My mouth fell open! I cannot *even* explain how this affected my mind.

Victoria continued, "You know Lucifer haved musical instruments in his body. He was very beautiful. When he walked he maked very beautiful music."

I was speechless! I couldn't think of anything to say!

HOW MANY INSTRUMENTS

She was not deterred by the alarmed look on my face, but

continued, "The Teenage Boy, he haved a lot of musical instruments hanging on a little rope around his waist."

She said, "He even have one that wraps around his head."

I said, "Oh, you mean like a Tuba?" She just looked puzzled because she had never heard the word Tuba. She just changed the subject.

WRAPPED AROUND HIS HEAD

The next day we drove to a football game in Brooksville. Another of my granddaughters invited us to come because she was the captain of the cheerleaders and it was their first game.

When the band played at half time, the Tuba player marched out on the field and Victoria said, "Majo that is it! The Teenage Boy... he plays one of them."

BRAIN STRAIN

Victoria had a great time watching the band play. I was still absorbed with the conversation we had the day before. I had not questioned her about Lucifer's robe. I could not believe I had actually heard that. I had to put it out of my head and enjoy the game.

As we drove back home it was on my mind again. That entire group of conversations about Lucifer's robe had stretched my mind to the max. I felt as though my head was a big balloon full of water and was bulging out both sides. I couldn't get it out of my head. I walked around for days with my brain hanging out of my ears. I couldn't get my mind around it.

LUCIFER LOVED GOD?

I had never even thought about the time when Lucifer still loved God. Now I couldn't *stop* thinking about it.

There was a time when Lucifer loved God!

BRAIN IS BETTER

My brain finally accepted it and one day I broached the subject again. I asked Victoria when she found out about Lucifer.

She said it was when Gabriel and Michael came to our bedroom and taught her from the "big book about the beginning of life." They let her see Lucifer when he was beautiful.

She has known about this since she was five and a half years old!

They let her see Lucifer in his beautiful robe when he still loved God. She saw all of his musical instruments and heard the beautiful music he made.

I had no idea that there was much more to come in the days and weeks ahead.

IN SEARCH OF A HORN

A few days later, I asked her about the old instrument. I asked her how old the instrument was and she said it was really, really, *really* old. I thought about that for a little while. She had *always* referred to it as an *OLD instrument.*

Could it be one that Lucifer played when he still loved God?

I waited and just thought about it. Then one day I asked her if it was Lucifer's instrument and she told me, "Well, yeah."

As if, I should already know.

I said, "How was it broken?"

She thought I meant what kind of damage did it have and she said, "it was just broke in two... " She held her fists out in front of her as though breaking a stick and said, "Boop! It was broke in two pieces."

I asked her when that happened and she told me it happened a long, long, ***long*** time ago. I asked her if it is possible that this instrument was broken when Lucifer fell from heaven.

She said in a matter of fact way, "Well, yes it was... I saw him fall from heaven."

Luke 10:18
And He said to them, "I saw Satan fall like lightning from heaven."

BIGINNING OF TIME

Victoria seldom gives us all of the details of heavenly experiences at one time. We learn a little bit here and a little bit there and then piece it together.

When we finally realize what she is telling us and ask her to confirm it, she just agrees with a, "Well, yeah." *We should know that already.*

It seems as though God tells Victoria how much to tell us at any one time. Perhaps if we were to hear it all at once our brains might explode.

LET'S PUT IT ALL TOGETHER

We know that one night shortly after she fell and went to heaven, Gabriel and Michael came to her and taught her from a really big book about "The beginning of Life."

This incident is in the book, 6 Big Angels.

She told us much later a little more about the big book.

I talked to Victoria and asked what came first, the big book or the bad place.

She told me that Gabriel and Mikey came to her in our bedroom ***before*** she went to the bad place and taught her from the book about the beginning of time.

She was going through The Fear of God School and was sleeping on a pallet on the floor beside our bed.

Some details that Gabriel and Michael showed her in the big book were about Lucifer... when he was beautiful.

They let her see Lucifer in his beautiful robe when he still loved God. She saw all of his musical instruments and heard the beautiful music he made.

They started at an earlier time when Lucifer was the Archangel of Worship...

MICHAEL, GABRIEL AND BIG BROTHER LUCIFER

Michael told her the three of them were best friends. They had lots of fun together.

They had races on their magnificent horses. Lucifer's horse was black.

She said, "Gabriel and Michael showed me something like a DVD that was in that big book... and I could go *in* there."

She said she was actually there with them for a while, when Lucifer still loved God, and they all had fun together. She even rode Lucifer's horse.

She continued, "Lucifer was actually kinda like a butterfly. He haved big wings like a butterfly that you almost can't see. They are very thin and beautiful.

"You could only see his wings real good when he was in the

glory of God, or in a rainbow. When he was with God or in a rainbow his wings was shinin' with all colors and changing.

"Nobody knows that he looked like a butterfly but me."

Victoria saw him as he walked in his beautiful gleaming white robe sparkling with gold and silver all over it. He had a belt on with all kinds of instruments.

When he moved his body and wings, it made very sweet and beautiful music.

Every move he made and every step he took was a sound of Worship and Glory. He led the praise and danced in the presence of God. She saw him when he was shining in his glorious beauty.

Her descriptions were vivid and detailed. She said "He have very beautiful, really long black hair. Sometimes he braids his hair.

"He haved a very beautiful smile and a beautiful little beard. He was so beautiful and his robe even haved all diamonds and rubies and all stones and jewels on it."

She said, "I saw his shield, with all beautiful instruments on him." She patted her chest so perhaps this could be like a breastplate that made music on his chest.

Then she added, "He could sing, too. He had lots of singing voice. High… low… medium… anything. He had ***every*** kind of voice. But not all at the same time."

I asked, "Did he sing really loud?"

She said, "Somehow (sometime) he sing loud and then not so loud but soft."

"Also", she added, "He haved gigantic hands, so he can play all the instruments.

"His boots haved like piano keys on them and he could stretch them out really long and play them."

MUSIC WITH AN ATTITUDE

She continued, "When he was mad at Jesus, he made really bad music and really bad drums."

His music changed while he was still in heaven.

"God gave Lucifer a spirit heart and it got 'turned around' and when he went down he had to leave his spirit heart in heaven and just go down with just his body."

FALL LIKE LIGHTENING

Michael told her about the battle in the heavenlies and Gabriel told her that Lucifer fell like lightening from the sky. They let her see it happen while she was in the big book like a DVD.

PATIENCE OF A FATHER

God waited a long time… thousands of years… to see if He would need a new Archangel of worship and then He decided that He did.

I asked her why God waited such a long time. She said it was to see if Lucifer would say, "I'm sorry." If he had said he was sorry, God would have let him come back. He still loved him even though he was "down there."

NEW ARCHANGEL

He made the new Archangel out of the spirit heart that stayed in heaven from Lucifer but God gave the new Archangel a regular heart that beats for Jesus.

I asked her if some of the praise angels had musical instruments in their bodies in a small way similar to Lucifer and she said yes.

Then I asked if maybe God promoted one of them to be the new Archangel of Worship.

She said, "What is promote?"

I explained that to be promoted is to be elevated from the position you are in and go to a higher position.

She said firmly, "No, God created him. He *is* the creator you know."

> 1 Thessalonians 4:16
> 16 For the Lord Himself will descend from heaven with a shout, with the voice of an archangel, and with the trumpet of God. And the dead in Christ will rise first.

> Rev. 4:11
> ... For you created all things and by your will they exist and were created.

I asked if she knows the new Archangel's name.

She said, "I can't quite remember... but he is much more beautifuller than Lucifer and makes more wonderfuller music.

"When he played the violin, he made me quiver. When he was playing the drums, he kept hitting himself 'cause he was part of the drums, not part of the violin.

"The new Archangel plays other instruments but have only drums in his body. When he hits his feet and legs... the sound bursts out. But it doesn't hurt him. (She actually said bursts, not busted)

"When he hits himself he doesn't hurt because he have like

a drum shield and so it doesn't hurt him."

CONSEQUENCES

Later Jesus took her to the Bad Place to let her see first hand the results of sin against God.

She saw the filth and slime that covered everything with a stench that made it very hard to breath.

She saw the ugliness of Satan and his followers. Things that she saw in that terrible place are still coming out little by little. She cannot talk about it for very long, it is so intense.

Victoria saw Lucifer get really mad when God created man and put him in the Garden of Eden on earth. He was so mad he decided to try to make man fall just like he did. He talked to Eve a *long, long, long* time before she finally ate the fruit from the tree.

Victoria has been giving us clues about all of this for a long time. A few months after she fell she told Uncle Carl about seeing the Tree of The Knowledge of Good and Evil.

Victoria has told her mom about being in the Garden of Eden *in Heaven* with Adam and Eve, and how beautiful Eve is.

She has recently been telling Mommy Bedtime Stories where she and Jesus go and relive incidents from the bible.

In one of the bedtime stories about Adam and Eve, she repeated to Sandi that she saw the Serpent talk to Eve for a long, long time before she ate the fruit.

The clues have always been there. We just failed to recognize the true meaning or significance of what she was telling us. I am positive that there is more to come.

I WAS WITH GOD A LONG, LONG TIME

Victoria first told this to Mommy when she was seven and a half. She told Sandi she was with God before the beginning of time.

> Jer 1:5
> 5 "Before I formed you in the womb I knew you,
> before you were born I set you apart;
> I appointed you as a prophet to the nations."
> NIV

One day He let her look at all the mommies in her world.

She saw her mommy and liked her best of all the people in her world.

Then God asked her, "Do you like her?"

Victoria answered, "Of course I do. She is decent and sweet and kind and loving."

Then God said, "Do you want her?"

She replied, "Of course I do. And He let me go and be in her tummy."

HEART TROUBLE

"Then when I was about to be born... my heart stopped beating and I went up to heaven."

I said, "**God! Don't let this happen now! I want to have my very own family.**

"Then God let me come back. And that's what happened to get me to this world."

Then Victoria started singing, "It's a small world after all."

She suddenly stopped after that one phrase and said, "It's not a small world, it's a **big** world.

I agree... Victoria's world is a very BIG WORLD!

HER WORLD IS GOD'S WORLD.

CHAPTER 8

LITTLE VICTORIA'S MOMMY

JUST A LITTLE VISIT WITH MOMMY

Victoria began talking more freely when she was almost seven years old. She began to explain some things that I never understood before. Some of the loose ends were coming together.

When we first heard about the babies, she told us they were squeezed out of their mommy before they were old enough to live.

She told me about a little baby that I knew. She was the grandchild of some friends of ours. They were hurt by the loss of their first grandchild to abortion. They told me about this loss just days before Victoria fell and went to heaven.

Victoria gave this baby her name, Victoria. She told us "Little Victoria was sad for a little and that she, Victoria, had whispered a little secret to her and made her feel better.

We knew about the secret that she whispered to "Little Victoria" but she wouldn't tell us what she said until some months later.

She cuddled this tiny baby against her chest and told her that if she missed her mommy down on the earth... she could come back with her and have a little visit... but she would have to hurry right back. This episode was related in 6 Big Angels.

We never knew if the tiny baby "Little Victoria" came with Victoria or not.

CHECKIN' WITH CHICKEN

I was sitting with Victoria in Chick Fil A in the autumn of 2005. I asked her if she still remembered the day she came back from heaven after she fell off our pool slide and she said she did.

Then I asked if "Little Victoria" came back with her that day and she said Yes.

She told me the angels took her and "Little Victoria" to see the tiny baby's mommy and then they came and brought Victoria back to us.

They each had a live angel animal in their hand. Little Victoria had a tiny pink teddy bear and Victoria had a little pink flamingo that one of the tiny babies had given her.

I thought Victoria was going to tell me more, and then, she just jumped up and ran into the children's area to play. She climbed around the play area for a while as I sat there proofing the first book, 6 Big Angels before sending it to the printer.

HAIR WE GO

I had just been reading about the wonderful descriptions of Jesus and His angels that Victoria saw in the top of her home church in Brooksville, Florida.

While we were just sitting there, eating lunch and talking, I asked her a question that I had wondered about... I was just curious.

I said, "Victoria, why did Jesus have brown hair at your church and "shine white" hair when you first saw Him in heaven?"

In a very matter of fact way she said, "Oh shoot, Majo, I saw Jesus' hair all kind of colors. I saw it pink and I saw it black...

I was so startled I could not get my food swallowed. Something caught in my windpipe and I was coughing violently. Victoria just continued to eat her chicken strips.

As soon as I recovered my voice, I asked, "Would you tell me what was happening when Jesus had pink hair?

JUST CLOWNING AROUND

She said with excitement in her voice, "Yes! It was a very happy time. Actually, it was Little Victoria's first birthday. We haved a party."

I was getting excited myself. This was something new. I had wondered about whether the tiny babies have birthday parties or not. After all, heaven is a place where time isn't exactly the same as we know it.

I said, "Wow! And Jesus came?"

Victoria's face was shining with happiness as she told me about Little Victoria's first birthday party.

PINK AND FUZZY

She said, "Jesus come with his hair all fuzzy and sticking out and shiny bright pink and He doo'd cartwheels and somersaults and danced and laughed.

"The Teenage Boy played happy music and Jesus juggled shiney balls. Jesus juggled with His hands and feet."

Incredulous, I asked, "Are you telling me Jesus came as a clown?"

She answered with laughter in her voice, "Yep! That's it! He was a clown. It was ***so much fun!***

"He was singing with us and we was singing and dancing. We haved a big, big bowl of ice cream. It looked like it was all vanilla, but I wanted chocolate... and then... when I dipped it into my bowl… it turned into chocolate!

"Little Victoria was so happy and I was, too. You know what, Majo?"

I said, "What?"

Victoria leaned back with a sweet smile at the memory and said with wonder in her voice, "Jesus could juggle with His knees... and He could *even* juggle standin' on His head."

I thought about Jesus as a clown for a moment and my heart just accepted it. I could picture the Lovely Lord that I know being a happy clown. Especially for these little thrown away babies who had such a rough beginning.

Actually, it is *just* like Him to do that.

JESUS HAS BLACK HAIR

We sat there and continued to eat in silence. I think she knew I was going to ask another question. She was already thinking about the time His hair turned black.

I was hesitant to ask about it. I waited a few moments and said, "Could you tell me what happened the time His hair was black?"

She said quietly, "That was a very sad time, a very, *very* sad time."

She continued with the explanation of the very sad time, "It was a very dark time and someone actually went down to the bad place. The demons actually came and put the rope around a man's neck and dragged him and pulled him until they got him down to the bad place.

"That is when Jesus' hair turned black just because he was so sad."

I said, "You mean His hair turned black from grief?"

She said, "Yes, that's it. Grief."

I said, "Who was the man?"

NATURAL AND SPIRITUAL

She said, "I don't know him and we couldn't see very well because when it happened a dark cloud came back and covered us and a black cloud was over us."

Two separate things happened: In the Spirit, a dark cloud came and covered them. In the natural, a black cloud was over them and it was raining.

Victoria continued, "It was me and Jesus and Little Victoria and The Teenage Boy." Then she added, "The Teenage Boy was playing very scared, sad music."

GOD'S WING

"Actually God covered *her* with his wing so she wouldn't be killed. He covered her to protect her so she wouldn't go down to the bad place."

I had a clue who she was talking about because she had mentioned Little Victoria. Then I asked if the girl that God covered with His Wing was Little Victoria's mother, Katy, and she answered, yes.

Katy was on the ground and God protected her with His wing. The man was on the ground and was dirty and they dragged him down to the bad place.

I asked, "Were there any angels with you?"

She said. "Oh yes, lots and lots of angels."

BLACK PAINT

When we got home, I went in search of a picture that Victoria had painted several months before with her watercolors. She had painted Jesus with black hair.

At the time she painted it, I wondered why she painted His hair black. I thought she didn't have brown paint or maybe mixed her colors and black showed up more than brown.

I just dated it and filed it.

We found the picture that Victoria had done in watercolors. It was in the art box in the office.

It was a picture of Jesus and He had black hair. I had a whole stack stapled together because she did them on the same day.

I had the date on the top one and on the bottom one. Don went on the internet and found when Katy was booked into jail.

Two weeks after the death of this young man, Victoria drew Jesus with black hair. That picture is on the inside of the back cover of this book.

I talked to Katy one day after that and ask her about that awful day. She told me that there was a really black cloud over them in the orange grove and it was raining.

She also agreed that everything Victoria said about that day was true.

WATCHING OUT FOR MOMMY

Katy is a very beautiful girl who has been running from God for many years.

This young girl has led a troubled life. Even though her parents' hearts are saddened many times, they love her and hold on to God for her safety and salvation.

The love of her little heaven baby has probably saved Katy's life many times.

This precious baby girl watches out for her mother and asks Jesus to protect her and He does.

STAKE OUT

Katy said that the night the police shot Jackie, and arrested her; the police had the house staked out and came after them.

Katy said she and Jackie had been there before. In fact, they had been there and stayed all night many times. This time they just went to the house to pick up some of his things.

She stayed in the car and Jackie went out to the shed and got his fishing gear. He needed to get into the house to get his clothes and other stuff that he had left there.

The guy who owned the house was in jail and they didn't have a key so Jackie went in through a window. He took a few things out the window and came to the car and they started to drive off.

POLICE CHASE

The police came around the corner about that time and followed them. The cops chased them and finally cut them off. They jumped from the car and ran through the brush into an orange grove.

Katy was running to hide behind an orange tree and the dogs went after Jackie.

IS GOD'S WING A COP'S FOOT?

She went face down on the ground. She either fell down or was knocked down. At that point someone put a foot in her back and kept her down. She thought someone hit her in the head.

She could have been killed by the police. I believe she fell and was kept down by an officer's foot. If she had been standing she likely would have been shot, also.

HOUNDS FROM HELL

The dogs dragged Jackie down to the ground. He had a sawed off shotgun in the back of his pants.

The police report said that as they were running out through the woods... the officer yelled for them to stop. The man turned with a shotgun in his hand and the police took him out. They shot him.

Katy said she did not believe he pulled the gun out but the police report stated that he did. However, Jackie was shot and killed and Katy went to jail.

DIFFERENT KIND OF WORLD

Victoria confirmed some stuff to us last year about where they were when she and Little Victoria saw Jesus with black hair.

They were down on the earth but in a *different kind of world.* Perhaps they were behind the veil?

MOMMY'S IN JAIL AGAIN

Recently Katy, Little Victoria's mommy, was arrested again.

She was not doing anything wrong. She was asleep in her mother's house, but she had been keeping company with a guy who had been accused of being involved in something illegal.

Katy was almost eight months pregnant when she went to jail. They combined this charge with the one when Jackie was killed and put her bail high.

Katy couldn't reach her parents because they had a restriction on their phone prohibiting unidentified numbers. For four or five days, she would call me from jail and I would dial her Mom in a three-way call and then let them talk.

She started losing weight... could not sleep for back pain, and was getting dehydrated and ill.

A LITTLE PRIVACY, PLEASE

I began to notice that Victoria was going into our prayer room and closing the door for two hours at the time. She often went in there several times during the day.

She told me, "I need to be private."

I had not put things together for the first four days because I was trying to help Katy get in touch with her mom.

I finally realized that Victoria must be seeing "Little Victoria" during those times in the prayer room.

I asked her. "Victoria, are you visiting with "Little Victoria" in the prayer room?"

She said, "Yes."

I said, “Has she been going to see her mommy?”

She answered, “Yes.”

I said, “You ***do*** *know* that her mommy is in jail, don’t you?”

She said, “Yes, I know.”

NO PRIVACY AT ALL

When Sandi got home from work, I told her about the prayer room visits, so she went into the back of the house and talked to Victoria.

She said, “Victoria, have you gone over there with “Little Victoria” to see her mommy?”

She admitted, “Yes, I have… and ... Mommy…? Why do they have to pee pee in the potty out there in front of everybody with just bars?”

Sandi asked her, “Is that what you saw?”

She said, “Yes, they have a potty and a little sink right out there with all the rest of the girls.”

Sandi asked. “What was the mommy doing when you and Little Victoria were there?”

Victoria said, “She was just sitting back on the pillows on her bed with her one leg kinda up there and one leg hanging off.”

The next day Katy’s parents were able to get her out of jail and I went over to see her.

SHE’S RIGHT, WE DO EVERYTHING IN PUBLIC

I asked about the bathroom and told her what Victoria had described. She told me, “She is exactly right. We have to do everything right there in front of everybody.

"I did sit with the pillows behind my back with one leg hanging off the bed most of the time."

She added, "All the girls that are pregnant and need to be close to the infirmary are kept in one big room. It was like one big horrible slumber party. Only you don't get to sleep."

I told her that her little girl was always watching out for her. I said, "Every time you are in trouble, she drags Jesus to you to keep you safe. She loves you and wants you to know that."

Katy said, "Thanks for telling me, Majo."

THE MESSAGE

I believe that many of the messages Victoria brought back from God are for restoring people who have been torn by the effects of abortion.

It touched Katy to know about her little girl in heaven and that she wants to help her.

Jesus felt compassion for the broken hearted.

> Luke 4:18
> He has sent Me to heal the brokenhearted,
> To proclaim liberty to the captives
> And recovery of sight to the blind,
> To set at liberty those who are oppressed...

We sometimes talk about why God could have given such a blessing to us, when we have sinned so much in our lives. He not only sent Victoria back to us but has sent us out to tell about the Knowledge of the Glory of God.

As Sandi said, we all have made mistakes, but God can use us anyway because: We are willing, we say "Yes" to whatever he asks, and we don't touch HIS GLORY.

God is using the mistakes we have made in our lives to bring healing to other hurting people.

We tell about "Little Victoria" everywhere we go.

God is using the story of Katy's little girl to heal women all over the world.

CHAPTER 9

BIG ANGELS AND BIG HORSES

STRONG WINDS

Four hurricanes packing very strong winds had swept through Florida within a twelve-month period of time beginning in 2004.

One of them slammed into Brooksville causing severe damage. At Sandi's house, the powerful winds literally twisted several big oak trees off above the ground and blew them over.

Sandi was watching out her window when she saw hurricane force winds whip the tops of the trees in what looked like a violent circle.

She was afraid the large oak tree close to her house would snap and fall on the roof. She heard a huge cracking sound followed by a heavy thud almost like an explosion as it hit the ground. She could not believe the tree had missed her house.

Later, her son, Patrick (Bubba) cut up most of the trees and stacked them in a big pile up against another large oak tree that was still standing. They were in 4 to 6 foot lengths and the pile was about 5 feet high.

PICKUP STICKS

Sandi walked out into her two-acre front yard to check on

Victoria. What she saw startled her and puzzled her. There had been a big pile of logs just a few minutes before and now, there was a scattered mess. Logs were all over the place.

Victoria was standing there looking around at a sight that looked like a giant had played pick up sticks with logs that were 12 to 15 inches in diameter.

This episode happened in the summer of 2005. Victoria was six and a half years old.

FACING THE KILLER

Earlier, Victoria had gone out into her front yard to play. She immediately found a wonderful thing... Bubba had made a nice pile of logs that were just waiting for her to climb up them.

She scampered up to the top of the logs.

When she got to the top, some ugly demons came rushing at her. There were a lot of them. They were trying to push her off and make the logs collapse and kill her.

She had no doubt they wanted to kill her.

THEY WENT THAT A WAY!

Sandi said, "OK, tell me what happened over there with the logs.

Victoria explained, "The logs went that way... that way... and ***that*** way," indicating a direction on the other side.

She was being evasive. She never liked to admit that the demons were after her again.

Sandi asked, "What were you doing on them?"

Victoria nonchalantly said, “Just climbing on them.”

Now Sandi asked bluntly, “Victoria, what happened? Was something trying to get you?”

Victoria hesitated because she just does not want to talk about demons, “They was... a demon. One hundred demons.”

Sandi said, “…and what helped you?”

Victoria answered, “The angels!”

Sandi pressed her, “So, they came and saved you when you fell on these logs... “

Victoria protested, “I didn’t fell!”

Sandi rephrased her question, “Well, when you were falling the angels caught you?”

THAT’S THE PITS

Victoria finally opened up, “Yep, they did.

“The angels come and catched me, and ***yanked*** me under the armpits.”

> Ezekiel 8:1, 3
> 1 While I was sitting in my house and the elders of Judah were sitting before me, the hand of the Sovereign Lord came upon me...
>
> 3 He stretched out what looked like a hand and took me by the hair of my head. The Spirit lifted me up between earth and heaven...

She was rubbing under her arms to show where the angels caught her.

Sandi started probing, "OK, and how many angels did you have today?"

Victoria answered very firmly, "One hundred angels and lots of big horses!"

Victoria started swinging her arm as though she had a sword in it and said, "They was doing like this and with a sword in their hands... and they was riding on a horse while they was fightin' demons."

Sandi exclaimed, "Wow, Victoria I bet they were beautiful."

Then Victoria added, "The demons have a hissy fit and they was kicking and throwing logs all over the place"

She continued the scary explanation of what happened as the logs began to fall.

SWINGIN' ON A LOG

Big angels and huge horses came swiftly to her rescue.

ROUND & ROUND WE GO

She said, "I was holding on to a log. A demon had the other end and he was movin' it.

"And then he was swingin' it round and round over his head, harder and harder.

"It was going faster and faster.

"I couldn't hold on, my fingers was slidin' off... and then I let go and I went flyin' up and zoomed up into the sky and a huge angel catched me."

This huge angel caught her high above the crashing logs that were falling and rolling.

A BLACK BEAUTY HEAVEN HORSE

He quickly flew over to one of the beautiful horses that had also come to her rescue. The angel tossed her onto the back of a huge black beauty Heaven Horse.

A large group of heavenly horses of different colors surrounded this beautiful black horse.

As Victoria related this to Sandi, she said, "The horses was just real horse colors, like brown, brown spotted, tan, white, grey, black spotted and a black beauty Heaven Horse.

"Not like *some other* Heaven Horses that are like pink and purple."

These mighty Heaven Horses galloped alongside the beautiful black beauty Heaven Horse that had her on his back. They made a protective shield all the way around her.

They zoomed up into the sky with her. As they traveled on up through the second heaven, the horses formed two columns facing each other with a space in the middle. They made a pathway between two rows of powerful heavenly horses standing on both sides shoulder to shoulder "like neighbors."

Thousands of huge Heaven Horses lined up side by side with their faces looking in, standing at attention. They were an impenetrable shield between Victoria and the demons that were after her.

These powerful horses and angels protected her from the many demons that were still trying to get through to attack her, the demons that occupy the awful domain of Satan in the second heaven.

Angels made a canopy over her and they took her on up, all the way up to the golden stairs and on up to heaven.

A MIGHTY BATTLE

Some very large warrior angels riding on huge battle horses stayed behind and fought the demons around Sandi's yard.

They wore armor and fought with swords, shields and lances.

When we come face to face with battles, all we have to do is pray and angels come and wage literal warfare right where we live. It is a fierce battle.

Make no mistake, Satan and his demons are after Victoria. She is a witness to the Glory of God in the earth, and a witness to the wonders of Heaven.

The angels won this battle, and then flew up and joined Victoria and the horses.

The logs were scattered all over Sandi's yard.

CHAPTER 10

WE WIN

RELIGIOUS TRADITION

In our first book “6 Big Angels,” we told about Victoria seeing Jesus on a huge white horse and His army on huge horses in the top of her church in Brooksville.

Victoria described in detail how the different ranks of angels were dressed and what their duties were.

The ones dressed in blue that were around Jesus were His Honor Guard. The next ones were in red and they blew on golden trumpets. The next ones also wore red and they were the singers. All the angels were on horses. The singers were men and women angels.

Jesus and the angels were through the roof and all in the ceiling of the church.

The top of the church was like an open heaven with no visible ceiling. This was an actual real time happening in the spirit that she could watch as it unfolded in her church.

Although Jesus was there, she saw demons on everybody in the church. They were “peein’, poopin’, and spittin’ balls of slime” on everybody there.

The first time she told us about these demons, the only people not covered with them were Pastor David Garcia, Victoria and Sandi.

GET OUT AND STAY OUT!

Even as the demons harassed them, Victoria fought valiantly to keep them off her and Sandi, and a wonderful thing was happening with Pastor Garcia.

Victoria said there were blue robed warrior angels on the stage and they were "just kickin' them demons right off that Holy Place."

They had recently moved into their new sanctuary. It is huge and shaped like a dome.

This church is totally debt free and poised to usher in a great move of God in Brooksville.

VISION & DIVISION

Pastor David Garcia has received a big, bold vision from God for this church. Part of this vision is for international outreach. He wanted to change the name of the church.

When we wrote about this church in our first book, it was the Brooksville Assembly of God, but was in transition. The Pastor wanted to name it Grace World Outreach Church.

The attack by demons was brought on by dissention and disunity. A faction of members and leaders opposed the change.

Those demons, "Dissention and Disunity," opened the door for "Strife and Backbiting." This brought in "Division."

The people in the church started taking sides.

STATUS QUO

Then those religious demons, "Pride and Religious Tradition" entered in all their pomposity and got very comfortable. They wanted everything to stay the same as it has always been. The name of their favorite program is "Status Quo."

This is what Jesus said when he came up against the Pharisees.

> Mark 7:6-8
> 6 He replied, "Isaiah was right when he prophesied about you hypocrites;
> as it is written: "These people honor me with their lips,
> but their hearts are far from me.
> 7 They worship me in vain; their teachings are but rules taught by men."

TRADITIONS OF MEN

> 8 "You have let go of the commands of God and are holding on to the traditions of men."
> NIV

That nasty little demon, "Fear of Change" was running around scaring everybody about what *could* happen if they changed *anything*.

This situation went on for about 5 months. Every time Victoria went to church, she saw Jesus and His army in the top of the church.

Demons were on everybody.

EAST – SOUTH – WEST – NORTH

In each service, Jesus, His horse, and all the angels were turned facing another direction.

The first time Victoria saw Him, He was facing East. Then He faced South. The next service He faced West and then the next service He faced North.

This continued for months. The demons were having a

good time. Then one Sunday, Grandpa and I just happened to be there when some of this stuff ended.

Some of the leaders and members who had opposed the pastor had repented. They got up and publicly apologized to Pastor Garcia and the entire congregation for their part in stirring up strife and division.

They accepted the name change and embraced the international vision of their pastor.

SEND YOUR ANGELS

Then Pastor Garcia prayed a wonderful prayer of thanksgiving to God for the unity that had been restored to their church. He asked God to bind the evil spirits and send His angels to fight the battle for this church, in Jesus Christ's Holy Name.

Victoria said there was a big fight and the angels came after the demons and ran every one of them right out of the church. The Lord has already won the battle. He fought this battle on the cross. He conquered hell and the grave when He rose from the grave.

There wasn't a single demon left in the church. It was a joyous day for The Grace World Outreach Church.

If you read the bible you know that in the end… We Win!

HITCHHIKERS

However, Victoria said the demons were waiting just down the road.

The battle was won that day, but not the war.

If anyone drove away from the church talking about the pastor or the deacons or anyone else in a critical way, they were just inviting the demons into their car.

The demons were looking for a place to go and they were quick to go where there was an open door.

IDLE WORDS

Remember, you can't recall words once they are spoken. Your mouth determines how your life will be, blessed or not.

> Matt 12:36-37
> 36 But I say to you that for every idle word men may speak, they will give account of it in the Day of Judgment.

BY YOUR WORDS

> 37 For by your words you will be justified, and by your words you will be condemned.

If anyone was critical of anything or anyone regarding the service, they invited the demons back.

Like so many others, this church continued to have problems with disunity.

The devil is desperately trying to destroy the vision and destiny of Grace World Outreach Church.

Pastor Garcia is standing firm in his resolve to fulfill the vision God has given him.

THE SEARCH GOES ON

In late 2005, Grandpa and I were asked to pray for the selection committee that was appointed to find the right person to lead the music for this season, for their church.

BIG ANGEL

Grandpa and I went out to the table beside the pool to pray. The big angel is always there, leaning against the sliding board where Victoria fell and went to heaven. I told Grandpa to punch me if he felt a prophetic word coming. I had the tape recorder ready.

We had communion and prepared to pray for the Brooksville church. As we bowed our heads, a wonderful anointing flowed over us. I pushed down the 'record' button.

This is part of the prayer. We flowed one into the other back and forth in perfect unity. We cannot even tell which part was me and which part was Grandpa because it was all Holy Spirit.

A PRAYER FOR THE CHURCH

This word of prayer was given to us as we were praying for this church. However, the substance of the prayer may be applied to many other parts of the body of Christ.

A SOLID FOUNDATION

> Lord, we come to you for this Brooksville Assembly of God.
>
> We know that You laid the foundation of that church many years ago and it's a solid foundation.

BREAK THE BOXES

> We ask that you open the eyes of the pastors and the leadership of that church and let them see what You are doing and what is coming by Your hand.
>
> We ask that you shred the boxes built by the traditions of man and occupied by the religious spirits… throw away the lids.
>
> Lord, fill this church with Your Holy Spirit, with Your presence, and the knowledge and manifestations of Your Glory.

RELEASE YOUR SPIRIT

We declare freedom in the church, release of Your Holy Spirit in every individual heart and spirit.

Lord, deliver the people from any demonic influence that is on them and give them complete freedom. We declare deliverance for that church.

Send Your mighty warriors, God, to fight for this church and burst it wide open with Your Mighty Glory and Presence, in Jesus Christ's Holy Name.

A BIG CHAIR

We recognize that we are in a war and we have been ill equipped to fight the battles. Prepare this church, that Your Power and the Might of Your Spirit will come down upon this church and equip the people for the war.

Let us not become captives. Let us not be afraid to enter the battle, but give us the courage in the natural and in the Spirit to wage war... with valor.

We ***know*** that the host of heaven led by Jesus Christ is waiting for the faithful to call them into battle.

Lord, you said You would inhabit our praise. We have to offer a big enough praise to hold You. You are so mighty, and huge. If we have a feeble praise and You come in, it would kill us… it would break us down.

It has to be a ***big enough chair*** for **You** to come and inhabit and abide and ***sit there*** and hover there with us and live in there as we praise You and Worship You.

Lord let us be strong enough to hold Your Mighty Presence with our praise and worship, Lord.

A BIG SOUND

Lord, we know that there is a new sound coming over the earth and it's a sound of war. It's a sound of mightiness. It's a sound of earthquakes and hurricanes and tornados and forest fires and tidal waves. It's a ***sound*** that's **violent** and the sound that's coming over the earth ***is for Your Glory***.

Most people will accept it and it is going to be loud. There will be lots of drums and bass guitars and trumpets and instruments of SOUND, lots of sound.

And the few people that pick up offence are going to need to humble their hearts before God and come on line because we are engaged in a war. This is a battle for the next great move of God.

People are going to come to God by the millions because of tragedy and judgment that is coming in the earth. The whole earth is being judged and people are going to be streaming to our churches for salvation. If we are not equipped what will we do? What will *they* do?

God, equip this church in a mighty way with Your Power and bring this new sound to the earth through Grace World Outreach Church.

A BIG FIRE

Let that great move of God start here, Lord. Let the people see a **COLUMN OF FIRE** over that church ***in the natural*** that they will be drawn by what they see ***in the sky over the church.***

Let Your Glory fill the temple. Rain down Your Glory Lord. Manifest Yourself so that there is no doubt that You are the ONE inhabiting the praise.

BREAK THE BOUNDRIES

Lord, give us signs, wonders, and miracles and manifestations of Your Presence that no one can deny. Break open the boundaries that we have set against Your manifestations.

Lord God, You have always manifested Yourself in a mighty way. You cannot BE there without manifestation. ***You ARE manifestation.***

We cannot stand in Your Presence.

Open the minds of the people in Your ministries that they will accept that You are going to do what You want to do, no matter what. You are so Mighty, Oh God, how can we think that we can tell you how you can manifest in our presence?

Lord, how can we think that we can tell You how long You can be in our service?

How can we even think that we can control what You are going to do for Your people?

OPEN US UP

Lord, open us up. Let us draw near to You as You manifest Yourself in our lives and in this church. Let there be no doubt that You are here.

Lord God, help them bring in the right person that You have for that church for their music ministry. Lord, send them the right one. Send them the one that you have ordained for that church.

Send them the one, the only one that You want there, for this time and this season oh Lord, for such a time as we are in right now.

Lord, use the foundation of this church as a threshing floor. We ask that You use Your winnowing fork to separate the wheat from the chaff.

Retain the good and dispel the useless so there is nothing left but fertile, wholesome, nourishing grain that will feed the body, Your Body of Christ.

Thank You, Oh God, In the Name of Jesus Christ. Amen

TOTAL PRAISE - TOTAL WORSHIP

As the selection committee interviewed their list of prospective music ministers, one stood out. He spoke many of the same words that were in the above prayer. He spoke of new sounds and big praise. He prophesied that people would say, “Have you heard the Brooksville Sound?”

They chose this man to be their new Minister of Music, Carlton Burgess.

GOD HAS A FLAG

One Sunday night in early April 2007, Sandi called on the way home from church and told me that it was an awesome service and Victoria was sharing with her about what she saw in the service.

They usually don’t have church on Sunday night, but Pastor Garcia and the new music minister, had planned this service to be totally praise and worship time.

As they sang, the glory came down and they worshiped God with singing, dancing and waving the flags.

After they got home on Sunday night, Victoria called me on the phone, and told me what she saw...

She said that God was dancing in front of the church and He was waving a very big flag that had animals on it. I mulled over the flag with animals on it for a long time. What was that?

GOD'S BANNER

The next day as we were taking a break from school, Victoria and I were talking about the service. She tried to explain what she saw. She saw God up at the front of the church dancing. His hair was flaming fire. His eyes were fire. His clothes were aflame. Everything was fire! **HE WAS ONE HUGE FLAME!**

He was waving a "*Humongous, Gigantic, Ginormous*" flag. This is the first time she saw God with a banner.

She said, "That flag was *humongouser* than any flag I ever saw."

BANNER FOR THE PEOPLE

> Isaiah 11: 10
> 10 In that day the Root of Jesse will stand as a banner for the peoples; the nations will rally to him, and His place of rest will be glorious.
> In that day the LORD will reach out His hand a second time to reclaim the remnant that is left of His people.

BANNER FOR THE NATIONS

> Isaiah 11:12
> 12 He will raise a banner for the nations and gather the exiles of Israel;
> He will assemble the scattered people of Judah from the four quarters of the earth.

FOUR QUARTERS OF THE EARTH

Remember Jesus and His angels in the top of the church.

They are looking in another direction every service. East... South... West... and North, to the four quarters of the earth.

ANIMALS?

Now Victoria began to explain about the animals on the flag. The flag was thin and flat, like real material used to make real flags.

The animals were flat like a picture but Victoria said they were alive and moving.

I asked her what kind of animals they were and she told me, "There was a Lion and horses with flames on them."

It looked like a movie on the flag with the Lion and the horses moving.

I felt better about the animals now that I knew what they were. The Lion could depict Jesus and the Horses with flames could indicate the Holy Spirit running free... out of the box.

OUT OF THE BOX

The Holy Spirit is ***out of the box*** and **running free** as ***Powerful, Flaming Wild Horses.***

The church, the body of Christ has had Holy Spirit in a box for many decades. I believe that the people of God are becoming so hungry for more... He has burst out of the box and has begun to run free.

Victoria saw God's throne just over the building. She also saw the "four faces" or Living Creatures.

Fiery angels filled the building. **Flaming Wild Horses** were racing through the people causing whirlwinds of fire to spin off as they ran.

2 Kings 2: 11-12
11 And it came to pass as they still went on and talked, that behold there appeared a chariot of fire and horses of fire, and parted them both asunder and Elijah went up by a whirlwind into heaven.
12 Elisha saw it and cried out, “My Father! My Father! The chariot of Israel and the horsemen there of.”
KJV

ARMY OF JESUS

Jesus and His army have been seen by Victoria in the top of this church since May 2005. He looked normal, with brown hair. Victoria couldn’t even say for sure that He had “fire eyes.” She said that He was way up in the church and she couldn’t be sure.

On this night of pure worship Jesus was still in the top of the church with His army. However, His eyes, hair and clothes were also flaming. He was one big fire. Jesus, like God, was a huge flame of fire.

The change in His appearance is very important. ***He is a flame of fire now. This church is ready for fire.***

MICHAEL’S ARMY

In that same service, she saw Gabriel and Michael. Each one of them was on a huge horse. They had flames all over their clothes and hair.

All around the inside of the building were “Cop Angels” who are the army of Michael.

Gabriel and Michael went and stood one on each side of Pastor David Garcia. Then they went and stood on each side of the Music Minister, Carlton Burgess. They went and stood on each side of the sound tech, Victoria’s uncle and then they went and stood beside the singers and musicians. Finally, they went and stood one on each side of Sandi and Victoria.

I believe Gabriel brought a message of world portent, a global commission, and Michael was sent to protect the message.

I believe part of the message was to the music. I believe Gabriel brought a message of knowledge of ***new songs*** and ***new sound*** to be birthed from Grace World Outreach Church. A sound to **be heard** around the world.

ANGELS ON R & R

Victoria said she saw a "thousand" wounded angels lying down on the floor in front of the platform. They were being restored by the praise and worship pouring out to God from pure hearts that were in unity before Him.

Remember what Pat Holloran, a Seer and Prophet, told me in 2005 about the wounded Angels. "They seek out a church with pure worship from pure hearts and lie down in front of the music and find restoration."

PURE HEARTS PURE WORSHIP

As this church continues in this kind of pure worship, many angels will be coming to Brooksville for restoration.

The pure praise and worship going up to heaven in unity from this church will result in something very powerful.

This will be a safe haven, established for the many Warrior Angels fighting the powers of darkness over Florida.

Grace World Outreach Church... a Heavenly Rest Stop.

ANOTHER PROPHETIC WORD

Just three days after the wonderful praise and worship

service on Sunday night, Prophet Chuck Pierce spoke at Grace World Outreach Church.

At the beginning of the service, he had a prophetic word for Pastor Garcia.

He said, “Every body stand and point at Pastor Garcia.”

Then he spoke these prophetic words.

> Over the last seven years I’ve seen that you’ve been... I saw it like this... you've been picking up sticks.
>
> You’ve been having all you needed to do. But the Lord is telling you these next seven years I am going to accelerate. The Lord said I'm going to show you how to start multiplying, and a multiplying anointing is going to rest in this place.

FIRE IN THE HOUSE

> But, I say to you I am going to have a ***FLAME OF FIRE*** rest upon the top of this dome, and that fire is going to start calling many in that would not normally come in. Saith the Lord.
>
> The Lord says lots of changes are ahead in this place, but I say to you, **my fire will begin to surround this area.**
>
> I will call people from a 150 mile radius to come and experience the fire that I am going to release. It will be known and it will be heard **that fire has rested on this place...** that **fire** is in **this** place.

HEAL THE BONES

> And I say that I am going to do a supernatural work to **heal the bones** of my people in this place. And

the Lord says there will be a healing breakout that occurs in this house and I say bones will be healed.

Blood systems will be healed.

I say to you **I have chosen this place** for a time such as this. Get ready for my move that **will overtake you**.

Let's just thank God for what He is going to do here. Wow! Awesome, awesome, awesome! Now Father I just say that this will be prepared, Father this is a place that **is prepared for visitation**.

The worship will be ready to lead into visitation.

THERE'S A FIRE IN THE HOUSE

As Chuck continued with the message, Victoria saw the church totally engulfed in flames. Even after the service was over when she went outside with Grandpa, the flames were still there.

Victoria looked up into the sky and pointed her finger up to streaks that were across the sky. She told Grandpa that it was the smoke from the fire that was on top of the building.

It looked like smoke that had come up out of a huge chimney and the wind had blown it sideways in a long streak across the sky.

It was a long trail of vapor and grandpa saw it. Victoria said it was the smoke from the fire that went all the way up to the sky.

She went and touched the outside of the dome and said, "It's still warm." She was touching the Dome at ground level.

During the service, she saw Flaming Wild Horses and Flaming Angels.

SPECIAL DELIVERY MESSAGE

When we got home from church that night I wrote down on a piece of paper what Victoria told Grandpa.

The next morning we went back to the church to attend the leaders meeting that Chuck was conducting. Victoria ran in and gave the piece of paper to Pastor Garcia.

After Victoria and I sat down in the pew, Pastor Garcia and an usher came to get us.

Pastor Garcia went ahead of us up the aisle as the usher helped Victoria and me to the back of the church. As we stepped into the hallway, Pastor Garcia beckoned us from the book table.

Victoria and I went down the hall and Pastor Garcia introduced us to Chuck Pierce, the Prophet. Pastor Garcia had already told him that Victoria saw the fire on the building and had given him our book, 6 Big Angels.

A SPECIAL PRAYER

Chuck shook hands with her, and said, "Victoria, I saw the same thing you did. I also saw a column of fire reaching from heaven to the top of the church. I sense that you have a gift for seeing. May I pray for you?"

Victoria shrugged her shoulders, and then shyly nodded. Chuck laid his hand on her head and prayed,

"Lord, I thank you for Victoria. Father, we ask you to give her clarity of vision. We ask you to give her the interpretations of what she sees and give her the boldness to speak it out. In Jesus name, Amen."

As Chuck preached that morning, he mentioned the music minister, Carlton Burgess several times.

He stressed the importance of the **new music** that is beginning to pour forth from Brooksville.

ON THE BRINK

Grace World Outreach Church is on the brink of an outpouring. It could start with the music. People will come from all over the world to hear the heavenly music at Brooksville, Florida.

I wonder if the song that starts it will be about the Fire on the Roof.

CHAPTER 11

GREAT CROWD OF WITNESSES

KID KONNNECTION

When Sandi decided that we would home school Victoria, we put her classroom in the room that we use as a prayer room. Half of the room is schoolroom and the other half is prayer room.

The school year started in August and on the first day of school, I set up our routine so it would be like going to school.

My plan was to ring the little bell, then open class with roll call. We would read from the bible and have prayer followed by a short segment of American history. We would end the routine with the pledge of allegiance and sing the Star Spangled Banner.

The first day of school, we had a surprise. As soon as I began the opening routine and called Victoria's name she quickly answered, "Here!" then she added, "Uhhh... Majo?"

I answered, "Yes, Sweetie."

She said, "There are nine other kids here."

I drew a deep breath and asked cautiously, "OK... Victoria... are these kids we know? Like, maybe the ones you already told us about at the Baby Place?"

She said, "Well, some of them are… but there are two new babies."

I carefully started writing down the names, ages, and descriptions of the children that I knew. We had seven of the kids she met on her first trips to heaven and two little tiny babies.

She said, "Majo, they don't have a name. We need to give them one."

This became a pattern of days to come. Every day as we opened school there would be more babies and children to name. Soon my roster had over a hundred kids listed and named. On many of the lines of the roster, I had where they were from, a description and why they were in heaven.

SALLY'S BABIES

One day Victoria said, "Majo there are two girls here and they are over *twenty* years old. She was looking up from her chair as though looking at a grown person. She continued, "They don't have a name either, can we name them?"

I had finished enrolling for the day, but went ahead and pulled out the roster and wrote down how they looked. They were sisters, but not twins and they both had blonde hair and blue eyes. I gave them a name.

We went ahead with school and after we finished for the day, Victoria wanted to go see my friend, Sally, who has rabbits, chickens and geese.

It is a long drive out into the country and Grandpa didn't really want to do it, but Victoria was quite insistent.

She said, "Grandpa, the children want to go see the animals really bad."

We called to see if she was home and asked if we could come out. She was delighted to have us. She knew about our classroom and understood that we would have many kids from heaven with us.

We piled into the Suburban and started down the road. As soon as we turned out onto the main road, Victoria said, "Majo, we need to stop at a store and get some Christmas lights and decorations for Sally."

Grandpa pulled in at a drugstore on the way and Victoria and the kids went in with him.

They came out with a nice box of Christmas lights and a pretty round container full of silver Christmas tree balls.

Victoria said the kids wanted to take them to Sally. The kids wanted her to put them on the outside. They wanted to be able to find her again, so they could come back.

We drove up into the yard and Sally came out to meet us. I handed her the lights and told her the kids insisted that we get them. I told her what the kids said about putting them on the outside so they could come back to see her again.

She started crying and told me she had not decorated her house in many years. A religious lady had visited her at Christmas time four years before and told her she should not be doing that because it was a pagan ritual.

I told her that I don't know the origins of the tradition of decorating and having a tree, but I love it. I think it is a good way to celebrate Jesus' birth.

The children and Victoria ran down the yard to the rabbits and we stood there watching. I turned to Sally and said, "We had two grown up girls today."

Sally said, "Do you think it could be my babies?"

When she was a young mother, Sally had miscarried a baby and almost died. When she became pregnant again her doctor insisted on terminating it because of her physical condition.

I said I didn't think so, Victoria just said they were over twenty. Then I asked how old her kids would be.

She said they would be around thirty five and thirty nine. She asked what they looked like and I told her they both had blonde hair and blue eyes.

I was standing there looking at a lovely lady with blond hair and blue eyes and telling her I didn't think they were her kids. I thought they were the wrong age.

A couple of days later it hit me. They would only look grown in heaven they wouldn't age past that. To Victoria they looked older than teenagers but the way she described it was "over twenty." She only guesses their age by the way they look.

I called her and said, "Sally, please forgive me, those had to be your girls, I was just stuck on the age thing."

She said, "I know it, Honey, I have already named them. I feel them here with me sometimes. I named them Juliana and Maria. Thank you so much for giving Christmas back to me."

I said. "Sally, it wasn't me, it was your beautiful daughters that gave Christmas back to you."

I told her I would change their names on my school roster. But a funny thing... Victoria didn't mention them again. I suspect they don't go to school here anymore.

I believe they came to us so Victoria could tell their mom about them. They wanted *her* to name them. I believe they are having a good time with their mother and all those animals.

DANCE PARTY

One day we were taking a recess break in the back family room. Victoria put on a praise CD and started dancing. She had on a long skirt and had a long scarf she was whirling around over her head.

She suddenly stopped and looked around the room. She told me that a hundred new babies and kids had just come into the room. I told them they were welcome to stay, but I couldn't name them all today.

She started dancing again and as she twirled, she said all the babies and kids were dancing, too. As she danced, I took pictures. When we looked at them in the view screen there were little tiny dots of light all over the pictures.

The next day I named ten children and babies. I had talked to Victoria about how much time it took away from our class and we decided to limit it to ten a day. If I didn't limit it... I could name babies all day long.

They really want their own mom to name them. But they told Victoria that they would like me to be their grandmother and I guess it is all right for me to name them. I told them that it is an honor to be their grandmother.

THE GLORY OF HEAVEN

This is just another aspect of the Glory of heaven come to earth and that is the Great Cloud of Witnesses.

> Heb 12:1-2
> 1 Therefore we also, since we are surrounded by so great a cloud of witnesses, let us lay aside every weight, and the sin which so easily ensnares us, and let us run with endurance the race that is set before us,

> 2 looking unto Jesus, the author and finisher of our faith, who for the joy that was set before Him endured the cross, despising the shame, and has sat down at the right hand of the throne of God.

The thing we did not understand before Victoria fell and went to heaven is that there truly is a cloud of witnesses with us at all times.

When we have communion with Victoria, the heavenly children are with us.

When we are in the classroom they are there. We still have to name new kids that show up for school.

When we travel we are accompanied by the children. Little Victoria and The Teenage Boy are almost always with us. Most of the time there are many others.

The children are always with us.

We live our life surrounded by The Great "Crowd" of Small Witnesses.

CHAPTER 12

WHAT WILL THEY THINK OF NEXT

Victoria has seen things in heaven that I definitely had a problem accepting. I've mentioned before that I would be comfortable with white robes, sweet music, the River of Life and a bunch of angels with harps.

As you will see now, our expectations and visions of heaven are a far cry from the reality. Now that I am getting somewhat used to the things we've been learning about heaven, I realize that we are looking forward to a really fun-filled eternity.

A RED SPORTS CAR?

In 2005, before we went to print with 6 Big Angels, Victoria told Sandi something that surprised her. She said, "Granny have a Red Sports Car." Sandi called me right away and told me what she said.

I did not even write it down or respond to it. It sounded almost irreverent to me. A car in heaven?

Please, just give me some harps and clouds!

YOU'VE COME A LONG WAY, BABY!

Then one day Grandpa and I were driving through Brandon with Victoria in the back seat. She looked out the window as a small red convertible drove up beside us and said, "That's almost just like Granny's car in heaven."

I gave Grandpa an exasperated look… and he just grinned. He had *never* had a problem with Granny's red sports car.

I *did* have a problem with that idea. I just could not seem to shake the idea that heaven is similar to Jerusalem when Jesus was there. At least heaven is ***way*** too holy to have fun stuff like a car.

I had known about this car thing in time to put it in the first book but I did not do it.

We have come a long way, Baby!

I have included some things now that I could not accept, then. Her revelations of heaven continue almost on a daily basis. Now we cannot wait to hear more about the exciting things to expect when we get there. We also pray for an increase in our ability to see into the spiritual realm.

BAXLEY, GEORGIA

We were driving to Baxley, Georgia for our second speaking engagement at El Shaddai Worship Center.[11] The Lord moved on us to share some of the unusual and sometimes startling things Victoria has seen and told us about in heaven.

I was reluctant. It is one thing to sneak stuff into the middle of the book but quite another to share it face to face with a congregation.

We started digging in the word and found some scriptures that surprised us. We read with our new eyes that are filled

---

[11] Pastor Ila Mae McLeighton
El Shaddai Revival Worship Center
Blackshear Hwy
Baxley, GA 31513

with the Knowledge of the Glory of the Lord. We could see clearly that God is an engineer.

HEAVENLY ENGINEER

There is evidence in the bible that God downloaded His designs to people in the earth for them to implement here. He literally provided a *blueprint* for what He wanted built here on earth. The Holy Spirit showed us examples in the scriptures.

When He instructed Noah to build the Ark, He provided all the information that was required to get the job done. That account is detailed in the Word.

Grandpa is an engineer and he told me it sounds like God provided Plans, Specifications and a Scope of Work.

BUILD AN ARK

> Gen 6:14-17
> 14 So make yourself an ark of cypress wood; make rooms in it

LINED WITH PITCH

> And coat it with pitch inside and out.

HEAVENLY BLUEPRINTS

> 15 This is how you are to build it:
> The ark is to be 450 feet long,
> 75 feet wide and 45 feet high.

ROOFING SUB-CONTRACTOR

> 16 Make a roof for it and finish the ark to within 18 inches of the top.
> Put a door in the side of the ark and make lower, middle and upper decks.

The detail of how to cover it inside and out with pitch was to keep it from leaking and sinking.

BUILD A LITTLE ARK

Later He placed in the heart of the mother of Moses details of how to build the little Ark to save the infant from being killed by Pharaoh.

BLUEPRINT FROM GOD

We have to believe that she was instructed to put pitch inside and out, like Noah, to keep it from sinking in the river.

> Ex 2:1-4
> 2:1 Now a man of the house of Levi married a Levite woman,
> 2 and she became pregnant and gave birth to a son. When she saw that he was a fine child, she hid him for three months.

LINED WITH PITCH

> 3 But when she could hide him no longer, she got a papyrus basket for him and coated it with tar and pitch. Then she placed the child in it and put it among the reeds along the bank of the Nile.
> 4 His sister stood at a distance to see what would happen to him.
> NIV

BRING AN OFFERING FROM A WILLING HEART

After God freed His people from the bondage of Egypt, He instructed Moses to build the Ark of the Covenant and the tabernacle. He downloaded Plans, Specifications and a Scope of Work with detailed instructions.

> Ex 25:1-9
> Then the LORD spoke to Moses, saying:

2 "Speak to the children of Israel, that they bring Me an offering. From everyone who gives it willingly with his heart you shall take My offering.

BILL OF MATERIALS

3 And this is the offering which you shall take from them:
gold, silver, and bronze;
4 blue, purple, and scarlet thread,
fine linen, and goats' hair;
5 ram skins dyed red,
badger skins,
and acacia wood;
6 oil for the light,
and spices for the anointing oil
and for the sweet incense;
7 onyx stones,
and stones to be set in the ephod
and in the breastplate.

SPECS

8 And let them make Me a sanctuary,
that I may dwell among them.
9 According to all that I show you,

BLUEPRINTS

that is, the *pattern* of the tabernacle and the *pattern* of all its furnishings,
just so, you shall make it. (*He means precisely. Do not deviate from the Specs or substitute materials.)*

THE ARK OF THE COVENANT

10 "And they shall make an ark of acacia wood; two and a half cubits shall be its length, a cubit and a half its width, and a cubit and a half its height.

LINE IT WITH GOLD

11 And you shall overlay it with pure gold, inside and out you shall overlay it, and shall make on it a molding of gold all around.

SCOPE OF WORK

12 You shall cast four rings of gold for it, and put them in its four corners; two rings shall be on one side, and two rings on the other side.

GOLDEN POLES

13 And you shall make poles of acacia wood, and overlay
them with gold.
14 You shall put the poles into the rings on the sides of
the ark, that the ark may be carried by them.
15 The poles shall be in the rings of the ark; they shall
not be taken from it.
16 And you shall put into the ark the Testimony which I
will give you.

MERCY SEAT

17 "You shall make a mercy seat of pure gold; two and a
half cubits shall be its length and a cubit and a half its
width.
18 And you shall make two cherubim of gold; of
hammered work you shall make them at the two ends of
the mercy seat.
19 Make one cherub at one end, and the other cherub at
the other end; you shall make the cherubim at the two
ends of it of one piece with the mercy seat.
20 And the cherubim shall stretch out their wings
above, covering the mercy seat with their wings, and
they shall face one another; the faces of the cherubim
shall be toward the mercy seat.

CONTRACT

> 21 You shall put the mercy seat on top of the ark,
> and in the ark you shall put the ***Testimony*** that I will give you.
> 22 And there I will meet with you, and I will speak with you from above the mercy seat, from between the two cherubim which are on the ark of the ***Testimony***, about everything which I will give you in commandment to the children of Israel.

HIGH TECH HEAVEN

In recent history this earth has been blessed with many inventions that have made our lives more enjoyable, easier, more productive and safer.

The thing we do not often think about is that every thing we enjoy here on earth had its beginning in heaven.

All that we have now, all that came before us and all that will come after us was in heaven before we saw it on earth. Every invention already has its prototype in heaven.

> Eccl 3:14-15
> 14 I know that everything God does will endure forever; nothing can be added to it and nothing taken from it. God does it so that men will revere him.
> 15 Whatever is has already been,
> and what will be has been before;
> and God will call the past to account.
> NIV

I believe the Holy Spirit began to reveal things to me about High Tech Heaven. As the timing became right for the earth to receive each new technology, He would release it over the earth.

He would release it to many individuals at the same time. That is why you read or hear about inventions that appear simultaneously at different locations; things like the light bulb, sewing machines, automobiles and television.

HERE AM I

I believe the Holy Spirit showed me that some people carried a Shield of Faith and had the willingness to receive what He had for them.

Some were willing but had a Shield of Self that they held over their brain. Those would believe the idea was of their own brilliance. Their self-knowledge was more important than anything else was.

> Matt 13:20-21
> 20 The one who received the seed that fell on rocky places is the man who hears the word and at once receives it with joy.
> 21 ... When trouble or persecution comes because of the word, he quickly falls away.
> NIV

Others received the download, but had the plan subverted by ideas instilled by the second heaven activity of Satan and his demonic forces.

> Matt 13:24-26
>
> 24 Jesus told them another parable: "The kingdom of heaven is like a man who sowed good seed in his field.
> 25 But while everyone was sleeping, his enemy came and sowed weeds among the wheat, and went away.
> 26 When the wheat sprouted and formed heads, then the weeds also appeared.
> NIV

I believe God downloads the ideas for technology to many people, but the ones who seize upon the idea have to possess the proper resume and qualifications.

First, they must be willing to say yes. They must also have:

Perseverance
Determination
Willingness to work hard
Ability to withstand ridicule
Fortitude to take risks
Willingness to sacrifice everything they have

Matt 13:23
23 But the one who received the seed that fell on good soil is the man who hears the word and understands it. He produces a crop, yielding a hundred, sixty or thirty times what was sown."
NIV

WHAT HAPPENED?

If all things had their beginning in heaven, why are there things like weapons of destruction such as nuclear weapons?

Everything was created with perfection in heaven and was downloaded in perfection. But remember that Lucifer was in heaven a long time with God. He knew many of the secrets of heaven and did not forget them when he fell.

When the new technology is downloaded to man, Satan has the ability to influence the person who received the gift. Many things that God meant for our good have been subverted in the second heaven for evil purposes.

Two powerful sources of energy we have are electricity and the atom. God used electricity in the form of created lightning a lot as described in many biblical accounts. The atom is His basic building block for every created thing.

What could have been a tremendous source of energy for our use has been usurped by evil people for destruction.

HORSE POWER AND ROAD RAGE

There is even evidence of automobiles in heaven. The world's first Hotrod is mentioned in 2 Kings.

> 2 Kings 2:11
> 11 Then it happened, as they continued on and talked, that suddenly a chariot of fire appeared with horses of fire, and separated the two of them; and Elijah went up by a whirlwind into heaven.

This scripture in Nahum sounds like it is describing the modern automobile.

> Nahum 2:3,4
> 3 The shields of his soldiers are red.
> The army is dressed in red.
> The metal on the chariots flashes like fire (Chrome)
> When they are ready to attack; (Road Rage)
> Their horses are excited. (Vroom, Vroom)
> 4 The chariots race through the streets (Late for Work)
> And rush back and forth (Rush Hour)
> through the city squares.
> They look like torches; (Headlights)
> They run like lightening. (Auto Race)
> *The Youth Bible, New Century Version*

Another version describes them this way.

> They shall rage in the streets (Road rage)
> They shall justle one against the other in the broad ways. (Fender bender)

I guess I have to admit that this Nahum guy must have seen cars somewhere. Maybe he also got a glimpse of "road rage" in a vision of the future.

HOT PINK MOTORCYCLE

Early in 2006 Victoria told us, "I have a Hot Pink Motorcycle in heaven and when I get on it… ZOOP… my clothes turn into a hot pink motorcycle suit."

She also told us that Granny has a red motorcycle that matches her red sports car. Then she added... Granny's red car is pulled by two beautiful white horses.

MOTORCYCLE ESCORT

Grandpa had just picked up Victoria at her Mommy's office in March 2007.

As they were traveling, Grandpa asked her if she still had the motorcycle in heaven and if it was still pink. She assured him that she did and she still rides it. Sometime she rides it here on earth.

Then he asked her if Granny still had her red motorcycle. She told him that yes she did. When he asked her if the horse that pulls her red sports car pulled it for her, she said, "No, Granny drives it herself. It is easier to steer than the car."

She told him that Granny does not drive very fast. She just goes "PUTT… PUTT… PUTT."

She said that Granny was driving her motorcycle right now, along side the car but was having a hard time catching up.

Victoria then acted out throwing a rope out of the car window to Granny's motorcycle and helped pull her along so she could catch up with them.

Then Grandpa asked her if Granny was riding on the road or up in the air. She told him she was riding in the air just above the road.

He said, "I guess this would be called "Float Ride."

She confirmed that, "Yep, she Float Rides."

Grandpa said, “I wonder if Jesus is riding on a Harley.”

Victoria responded as if he should already know that, “Oh brother! Well, yes! I’m looking at it right now. It is “humongous” and covered with fire.

Then she was grasping at the limits of her vocabulary to describe how big God’s Motorcycle is, “And God’s Harley… It’s “humongouser” than Jesus’ Harley. It’s got **lots** of fire.”

Grandpa said, “I bet they are going VROOM… VROOM… VROOM.”

Victoria, rolling her eyes, said, “Oh Brother… Yeahhh! I can hear them doin’ ***that*** right now!” And, she agreed, Granny was still going Putt… Putt… Putt.

Victoria has recently learned to roll her eyes and say, Oh brother.

CHARIOT OF FIRE

A friend of ours has some friends who had read her copy of our book 6 Big Angels and they wanted to come by and meet Victoria. We assured her that she would be here. She and the couple came on over the next day.

He has a powerful testimony and we spent the afternoon sharing wonderful supernatural experiences.

He had a terrible accident on his motorcycle during a time that he was running from God. He saw a flaming chariot come down. He miraculously survived the accident.

When we told him Victoria has a hot pink motorcycle in heaven, he started to grin and cry at the same time. It was confirmation to him.

The Lord had told him he has a flaming motorcycle waiting for him to ride as he enters the gates of heaven. He had been afraid to tell us about it because we might think he was crazy.

He told us about the Harley he has now. Twenty years after his accident the Lord provided him a new motorcycle, it was flaming orange with a flame design painted all over it.

He said the Lord told him, that was his Flaming Chariot.

We have many inventions in our lives that we accept as being created from man's ingenuity. Believe me; everything that is good, that is for our comfort and convenience is from God. Even our beds

GRANNY'S BUNK

When Granny was living with us she had an automatic adjustable bed that goes up or down with a remote control. Granny really liked her bed and so does Victoria, who had us put it in her room.

Sandi wanted to know if Granny ever comes to see her when she is in her bed.

Victoria said, "Yep, she does come and lay down on this bed when she wants to come see me... but she have a bed in heaven that goes up and down and she doesn't need a 'gremote'.

"She just speaks to it and it does what she asks it to do."

GRANNY'S COMMUNICATION CENTRAL

Victoria and Sandi were in the shower and I heard Sandi ask her how Granny's room looked.

She said, "It is really pretty with roses on the wall. She have flamingos in there. She have pictures of us on the wall. All of us... all of her family."

Sandi wrapped herself in a towel and came into the living room to tell me about the pictures.

I said, "I bet they are alive and not just still pictures."

Sandi went back into the bathroom and said, "Victoria, how do the pictures look? Are they just like these on the wall here at Majo's?"

Victoria said, "No, they move. Where ever you are or what ever you are doing she can see you. She can see you and me taking a shower together right now."

I can only imagine, but the pictures could be little portholes from heaven to earth and our loved ones can check on us and see how we are doing.

TUMBLING WITH AN ANGEL

We cannot always rely on technology to provide us with all of our needs. Sometime we just need divine intervention to help us.

Late in 2005 Sandi was trying to tie up some loose ends. She asked Victoria about an accident she had on Cousin Amy's little four-wheeler on Thanksgiving day, 2004 when she had just turned six years old.

Sandi asked her, "Did you call the angels, that day? You know, on the four-wheeler when you fell and crashed. Did you call out, 'help me Jesus... and help me angels?'"

Victoria answered, "Oh, that's the same thing. The angels save me again and again! Every time!"

Sandi recalled how bad the accident was. Victoria had been driving fast to keep up with the big kids. She hit a rock in the road and the little four-wheeler flipped over and over and Victoria tumbled over repeatedly on the white gravel road.

Everyone who saw it was running to phone 911, for an emergency crew.

It looked as though every bone in her body would be broken.

HOW COULD THAT BE?

Victoria quickly got to her feet and looked at her hands. She was astonishingly clean and fresh. She did not even have road dust on her. Not a single scratch or stone bruise. Her hair was not even dusty or full of trash. Nothing!

Sandi said to Victoria, "You didn't have a scratch on your elbow or anything… "

Victoria agreed, "Yeah… how could that be?"

Sandi asked her about it again, she said, "What did the angel do to keep you from getting hurt?"

She said an angel held her and wrapped around her body so she was like in the middle and wouldn't touch the ground anywhere. She said, "We just rolled like a ball until we stopped."

NO OTHER GOD CAN SAVE IN THIS WAY

> Daniel 3:26-27
> 26 So Shadrack, Meshach, and Abednego came out of the fire.
> 27 ...the fire had not harmed their bodies.
> Their hair was not burned,
> Their robes were not burned,
> and they didn't even smell like smoke!
> The Youth Bible, New Century Version

After the Hebrew children came out of the fiery furnace unharmed, Nebuchadnezzar said these words. "…no other God can save in this way."

Victoria has been saved from serious injury or even death many time by the angels sent to protect her.

NO LOITERING

Sandi checking to make sure Victoria remembered her instructions said, "And you know how to get the demons away from you too."

Victoria assured her mommy, "I know… say in the name of Jesus you have to go."

Sandi smiled and said, "That's exactly right. Do you say that a lot?"

Victoria said very firmly, "Yes... and the demons? They *still* have to go."

HEAD AND SHOULDERS

On the same tape at a later time, Victoria was either drawing or showing her mother how big God's shoulders are. Sandi said, "God has big shoulders like that?"

Victoria nodded and said, "He's scary."

Sandi said, "God's not scary!"

Victoria, who knew better, just made a noise, "Huh-h-h."

I'm sure she was thinking, *"If she only knew."*

Many people who have been to heaven express feelings of fear and awe at the tremendous magnitude of the **Power of God.**

> Dan 4:34-35
>
> 34 At the end of that time, I, Nebuchadnezzar, raised my eyes toward heaven, and my sanity was restored.

Then I praised the Most High; I honored and glorified him who lives forever.
His dominion is an eternal dominion;
his kingdom endures from generation to generation.
35 ... He does as he pleases
with the powers of heaven
and the peoples of the earth.
No one can hold back his hand
or say to him: "What have you done?"
NIV

Luke 12:4-5
4 "And I say to you, My friends, do not be afraid of those who kill the body, and after that have no more that they can do.
5 But I will show you whom you should fear: Fear Him who, after He has killed, has power to cast into hell; yes, I say to you, fear Him!

CONCRETE ANGEL

We ministered in Baxley on a Friday night and God blessed in a mighty way.

The next day we went to lunch together with a group of Ila Mae's family and friends, who are like family to us.

As we finished lunch and sat in the restaurant talking, Sandi and Victoria went outside with Ila Mae's daughter, Donna and her children. Victoria was running around on an old concrete parking lot that has gravel scattered on top of it.

As she ran, she tripped so hard her shoe came off and she pitched forward headlong. She tried to keep her balance but never made it. She did a belly flop on her hands, tummy and legs. The force of the fall caused her to skid along the pavement.

Sandi immediately ran and grabbed a bowl of ice water to put her hands in thinking she would have terrible road burn and scrapes.

Victoria said her hands felt hot.

Then she pulled them out of the ice water and looked at them. Her hands and arms were totally unmarred. There were no scrapes or even pinkness on her hands, knees or stomach.

Sandi asked Victoria if she saw anything and she said, “An angel was in the concrete stretched out on his back with his hands up over his head and he caught me with my hands in his hands and my body and legs landed on him.”

She concluded, “I wasn’t even hurt ’cause he caught me!”

CHAPTER 13

CALENDAR OF GOD

OF THE SEASON

During the writing of 6 Big Angels we were asking Victoria about how often she goes to heaven. She said several things about it.

She said, “Well... sometimes... I go back... and sometimes I don’t... because sometimes Jesus is very busy.”

Then she said in her deep voice of authority, “Sometime I go back ***of the season...*** *and also a little back.”*

Later, when she was almost seven years old I asked, “Victoria what did you mean that time when you said that you go up there to heaven, **of the season**.”

A NEW MONTH THING

She started trying to answer me and I wrote it all down. She gave me a number of statements that did not mean a lot to me at the time. They included the following one-liners.

It’s a celebration about how much people love God.

A day is like a month and a minute is like a day.

We celebrate Christmas when it’s not December yet.

Then she said, “Hanukah is something I love.

There is something like a new month thing.

There is one where we have pie throwing. We throw apple pies.

Then we have apple bobbing. I won three or four times.

The lemon pie was delicious. My favorite was pumpkin pie and strawberry pie. They had a lot of other pies."

At first, I thought she was describing one event and was going to include it in this book because she said some really cute stuff. I loved the one about a day is like a month and a minute is like a day.

WINE WITH JESUS

Recently I was reading a transcription where she told Mommy about drinking wine with Jesus.

I suddenly realized she *could* be describing Passover. Then I went back and looked at all the other statements she made concerning the "of the season" episode and was surprised.

I'm sorry to admit it, but I am not an expert on God's Calendar. However, I believe some of those statements *may* describe activities that happen at some of the Jewish Holidays.

That indicates to me that they observe the celebrations of God's Calendar in heaven.

PASSOVER

It was after her seventh birthday that Victoria told Sandi that she and Jesus had communion in heaven.

Sandi asked her if she drank wine.

Victoria answered and said that yes, she did.

Sandi wanted to know how the wine tasted.

Victoria said it tasted "kinda sweet but kinda sour." But she said she liked it. It was pretty good.

MATZOTH WITH A CROSS

Grandpa asked what the bread was like. Was it like the unleavened flat matzoth bread we use for communion or just a big loaf of bread?

She told us it was very large. It was round and very flat with "like a cross" on the top.

She said, "It have the cross just cut into it."

She said it was very large because a lot of people were there.

This is one of the times; she was in heaven, "of the season."

We believe they were celebrating Passover.

Recently I asked Victoria if they had other stuff to eat when she had wine with Jesus.

She said, "Oh, yes, we have meat that was very good. We didn't kill anything... Jesus made the meat and cooked it."

Then she mumbled softly to herself, "I don't know what kind of meat it was but it taste alright... it was very good.

"We have other stuff, too. But I can't remember."

PENTECOST

A friend of mine who was raised Jewish and then accepted Jesus Christ as the Messiah thought the first two statements may describe Pentecost. The law was given to

Moses fifty days after they were delivered from Egypt. It is a joyful time of celebration of God's abundance.

Victoria said, "It's a celebration about how much people love God."

"A day is like a month and a minute is like a day."

I asked Victoria about the celebration of Pentecost and she said they sung songs in heaven. Could they have been singing Psalm 90? The composer of this song was Moses, and it contains the words; For a thousand years in your sight are like a day that has just gone by. NIV

BEFORE WE KNEW

Early this year before I knew any of the revelations of God's blueprints and technology, I was trying to find out what happened in heaven when we were in Baton Rouge on the Feast of Trumpets or Roshashana last year.

I was still in denial about cars in heaven at that time.

FEAST OF TRUMPETS

I mentioned that we were in Baton Rouge with Sharnael Wolverton that night.

I said, "Do you remember when Sharnael asked a lady to come up and blow her Shofar?

She said, "Yeah, I think."

We had been to so many conferences, it was difficult for her to place which one I meant.

I said, "Try to remember when we were singing and dancing and blowing the Shofar. We were at the conference in Baton Rouge, Louisiana."

She still looked puzzled, so I continued with my explanation.

"It was in the evening and when the sun went down it began the Feast of Trumpets or the Jewish New Year..."

Her face cleared as I said Feast of Trumpets...

I concluded, "I was wondering if they were having a celebration in heaven that night?"

She said, "Yes, but I missed it."

I asked why she missed it and she said because we were at that conference.

TRAFFIC JAM

Then she added, "I tried to go later but the traffic was too bad."

I just looked at her blankly and she said, "If you don't think they have traffic in heaven, you better think again. By the time I got there the party was almost all over!"

DANIEL DISTRESS

I was so astonished, I instantly got a headache and my eyes felt as though they were going to burst.

> Daniel 10: 8
> I had no strength left, my face turned deathly pale and I was helpless.

Victoria brought me some water and I took two aspirin and put an eye cover on my eyes and the heating pad to my neck and head.

I felt a migraine coming on.

Grandpa came in to see about me and I told him that I was having a Daniel Distress attack. Sometimes your brain just goes into overload and you get pale and sick.

NEW JERUSALEM

As I lay there, with every beat of my heart pounding in my head and eyes, I went into a deep sleep. I saw a vision of the city of Jerusalem in heaven, The New Jerusalem. In my dream I was over the city looking down.

I saw people rushing to the City of Gold for the celebration from all over heaven. There were throngs of people.

> Daniel 7: 15
> I, Daniel was troubled in spirit and the visions that passed through my mind disturbed me.

MY CAR CAN'T FLY

Victoria was still beside me on the bed when I came out of it. I asked her if the traffic jam was because everyone wanted to be in New Jerusalem in heaven for the Feast of Trumpets. She said that was exactly right.

I was feeling a little better until she explained.

She continued, "I was doing OK, driving my red sports car, but then we couldn't move because of so many people.

"But my car is alive and can drive itself, when the traffic gets better."

Then she added, "But it can't fly."

MY HORSE CAN FLY

"I had two of my horses with me so I hopped on the white one and we flew over the traffic.

"But the party was pretty much over when we got there."

I pulled my eye cover back on and lay real still so my head wouldn't explode. I was thinking, *"I wonder if this is going to be the death of me."*

> Daniel 8: 27
> I, Daniel, was exhausted and lay ill for several days.

As I lay quietly for a little while, Victoria was busy drawing pictures.

She drew someone blowing a Shofar.

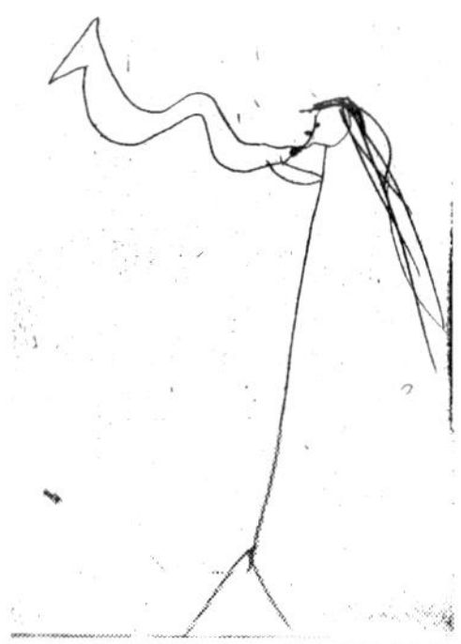

MAN WITH SHOFAR

APPLE DIPPED IN HONEY

She drew an apple that was very large with lines around it showing that it had been dipped in something. She said that was honey.

She brought the pictures to me and I removed my eye cover and looked at them.

APPLE AND HONEY

She went to the refrigerator, got a big apple and completely covered it with honey.

Blessedly it was on a plate. She carefully walked through the house dripping only a little honey on the floor.

I lay with my eyes closed. She came into the bedroom and handed it to me. I opened my eyes and saw that the honey was dripping over the edge of the plate. I was trying to sit up and steady the plate and was rendered speechless.

She paid no attention to my condition and said, “They dip the apples in the honey.

“The river of honey has a place that it comes into the building where they was eatin’ and it goes down the middle of the table. They just reach over and let honey pour over their apple.”

I understand from some of my Jewish friends that the apple and honey thing is always done at the Feast of Trumpets.

I suspect the apple-bobbing thing is an activity for the children at Feast of Trumpets.

TABERNACLES

Then she drew a picture of a hut that she said is made out of cloth and straw and wood.

HUT OR BOOTH

HANUKAH

Victoria specifically named Hanukah or the Feast of Lights as one of the feasts that she loves. We attended a Messianic Jewish church last year on Hanukah. Victoria was singing right along with everyone else in *Hebrew*. She said those were songs she learned in heaven.

PURIM

I have to admit she threw me a curve when she talked about pie throwing, but I just found out from someone who has been to Israel that they have very exciting parties at Purim. They hang up a canvas with a hole cut in it and a man sticks his head through it and pretends to be Haman. Everyone throws pies at him.

They read from the Book of Esther and every time the name of Haman is mentioned, everyone stomps their feet and makes rude sounds.

NEW MOON

The Jewish Calendar is a Lunar calendar. There is a celebration every month on the new moon. That would be the New month thing.

> Ps 81:3-5
> 3 Blow the trumpet at the time of the New Moon,
> At the full moon, on our solemn feast day.
> 4 For this is a statute for Israel,
> A law of the God of Jacob.
> 5 This He established in Joseph as a testimony,
> When He went throughout the land of Egypt,
> Where I heard a language I did not understand.

I have no idea about the lemon, pumpkin and strawberry pies, unless that is what they serve for dessert every new moon.

She said she has been to a lot of celebrations in heaven... probably 125 million... Then she summed it all up, "After all... I have been going up there for *two* years." *She has been going up there since 2003.*

I'm almost positive God isn't through with this subject yet and you can see, I really need to study up on this Calendar of God stuff because I'm sure God is laughing all over heaven at me.

I am convinced we will be hearing more about the Calendar of God in the future.

If I am able… I will write about it.

CHAPTER 14

BEDTIME STORIES

Bedtime is a very special time between Sandi and Victoria. That is when Victoria feels the safest. They snuggle in bed and have a good time talking about the people in the bible that Victoria has actually met.

She and Mommy read from her Bible Story Book and pray. That is when Jesus and the angels are very close. This is where we get so much of the information about heaven.

During these times Victoria is ready to share some really neat stuff with Mommy.

The following are talks between Sandi and Victoria when she was between the ages of six to eight years old.

ANOTHER FISH STORY

Sandi had just read about Jonah being swallowed by a big fish when Victoria looked up at her mommy and said, "You want to know what Jonah eated while he was in the big fish?"

Sandi, thinking it was a joke, said, "Well, sure I want to know what Jonah ate while he was in the big fish."

Victoria said, "He eated rotten fish."

Sandi went, "OH YUCK! Rotten fish! How do you know that?"

Victoria answered, "Because I was with Jonah when they threw him overboard. I was in the fish's stomach with Jonah!"

Sandi who shouldn't be surprised at anything any more... said, "You were in the fish's stomach?"

Victoria, with a satisfied smile said, "Yep… and that rotten fish didn't really taste that bad at all.

"There was something down there that was kinda dark looking and Jonah put that on little pieces of fish and it was a little bitter but not too bad."

Sandi was almost sick, "You ATE some of it?"

Victoria answered, "Well yes, I was hungry and that's all we had."

Victoria went on to explain how it felt to be spit out on the land... really yucky... and how they washed the slime off in the edge of the water.

Then they went on to that big city to preach.

HE GOT THE BIG HEAD

Victoria was eight years old, and was again telling Mommy bedtime stories.

She said. "I was with David when he killed Goliath.

"Goliath was yelling at David's brothers and all of the soldiers and I yelled back at him and told him to be quiet.

"Everybody looked at me.

"David looked so funny in Saul's armor. It was huge and maked him lean over a little.

"He tooked it off and then we walked down by a little stream of water and he picked up 5 stones. They was a little dry and a little wet.

"Then after the rock hit Goliath, he fell down and David ran and cut his head off with his own sword. There was blood spurtin' everywhere. It got all over the ground.

"That giant have a **very** big head."

JUST LION AROUND

She was with Daniel in the place where the lions were. She and Daniel leaned against a big lion with their heads on its stomach for a pillow, and went to sleep. The lions couldn't hurt them because of the angel.

STORMY WEATHER

Sand asked her if she got to be with anybody else.

She said, "You know that time the disciples and Jesus were in the boat and Jesus fell asleep... and the storm came... well I was there and the disciples were very scared and almost mad at Jesus."

She said, "They woke Him up and He made the storm stop."

JUST A STROLL IN THE DARK

Victoria continued, "You know that time the disciples were going across in a boat and they saw Jesus walking on the water? Well, I was walking on the water with Jesus.

"Then when He told Peter to come on out to us... and then Peter got scared and started sinking and I said, 'JESUS! SAVE HIM! DON'T LET HIM DROWN!'

"Jesus put one arm around me and patted me on the

shoulder and said, 'Don't be afraid, little one, I will save him.'

"Then Jesus reached out with His other hand and lifted Peter up out of the water and we walked together... Jesus... Peter... and me... on the water over to the boat and got in."

Then she added, "Mommy why was Peter a fisherman if he didn't know how to swim?"

Sandi said, "I don't know, Sweetie, I sure wouldn't work on a boat if I couldn't swim.

Victoria agreed, "Me neither."

ANYTIME YOU'RE IN THE NEIGHBORHOOD

She watched the man let down through the ceiling who was sick. She said he was almost dead.

Then when Jesus touched him, he rolled up his bed and walked out of there, praising God.

ON THE DONKEY WITH JESUS

She was on the donkey with Jesus as He went through Jerusalem. The people were shouting, "Hosanna! Hosanna!"

JESUS HAVE A WHIP

She said, "I was with Jesus in the temple when He have the whip. He was **sooo** angry!"

Then she appeared to be puzzled and softly said, "But He was whipping the temple and that is His own body. He was whipping the body... ***His*** body."

CATERED AFFAIR

She said, "I was the little boy with the fish and loaves of bread"

Sandi wanted to know more and asked, "You got to be with Jesus when He was with the disciples and He fed all those people?

Victoria got very excited as she responded, "Ohh yesss, I LOVE that bread! It was so good!"

Sandi asked if she ate the fish, too.

She replied enthusiastically, "Yep! IT WAS THE BEST FISH I EVER TASTED!"

Then Sandi asked her if she saw the little boy with the basket that the fish and bread came from.

*Sandi didn't understand that **she** was the little boy at this time, that Jesus was letting her see this miracle from the viewpoint of the boy.*

Victoria replied, "Yep. Even I was with Jesus evvv-ry where he went."

Sandi asked, "Yes, but didn't you see the little boy that had the fish and loaves of bread in heaven?"

MOVIN' ON

Her answer was a little odd as she replied, "Ya' know, I don't know, because there is all kinds of people up there."

Sandi could not keep up with Victoria. She was already moving to something else.

PUT THAT IN YOUR HAT

She continued "All kinds of little boys and little girls and do you know what? They have cool hats like this. It has little circles on it and they have it so I can put it on my head. I actually have one in my room up in heaven."

Sandi was puzzled and asked, "You have a hat in heaven?"

Victoria assured Mommy, "Yep! It has… it says... 'Jesus rules! Jesus rules! Jesus rules!' and then it says 'I love Jesus. I love Jesus.' Everywhere!"

I thought she meant that it was a talking hat, but she said no... she meant that the hat had cool stuff written on it, and then it changes and something else is written on the hat.

I wonder if the little circles are something like digital screens and the message can change to say different things.

I CAN SING

Victoria told Sandi, "Actually I have a song... Up in heaven."

Sandi wanted to know what the song sounded like.

Victoria said, "Ummm… OK... I can sing you the song... I know how the song goes because I been singin' it since the first thing that I got up there."

A COOL BEAT

She continued, "I know it really well... it have a part that's really cool. It have a part that goes…"

> **Hoof chugga choo, chugga choo, *choo* Ugh!**
> **Hoof chugga choo, chugga choo, *choo* Ugh!**

"Ohh… I just mess up that song."

She was trying to show her Mother the beat of the song. Sandi was surprised and said, "I would say it's got a really cool beat to it."

Victoria answered, "In the middle... like…"

> **Whew!** Huff huff.
> **Whew!** Huff huff.
> **Whew!** Huff huff… **Whew!**

Sandi asked her if she could sing it to her.

Victoria reluctantly said, "Oh alright."

She sang the following song.

> I have Jesus in my heart
> I have Jesus in my soul
> I have Jesus everywhere
> And I can sing all over there
>
> I have the cool hats
> I have the funny hats
> But I have wonderful
> Jesus everywhere

ROCK AROUND THE CLOCK

Victoria finished that night of bedtime fun with some Rock and Roll. She sang one more song to Mommy.

> Rock and Roll, Jesus!
> Rock and Roll, Jesus!
> Rock and Roll, Jesus!
> Rock and Roll, Jesus!
> Oh-h-h-h-h Yeah…
> Rock and Roll, Jesus!

She told Mommy, "Jesus likes Rock and Roll"

It was so much fun, Sandi joined in and they sung Rock and Roll Jesus for a little while.

Victoria said Jesus *loves* to dance to that song.

MIKEY IS BACK

When Victoria was seven years old, she was in the pool and I was sitting beside it. I asked her if she could still see her six angels.

She said, “Yes... sometimes.” She waited a moment and said, “Mikey is with them now.”

I said, “He is?”

Then I asked, “Is this the same Mikey who came with Gabriel and taught you from the book of life?”

She said, “Yes.”

NOW THAT’S A REAL FISH STORY

When she was a little past seven, Victoria and I were talking about the book 6 Big Angels and all the things she had told us about heaven.

I asked her if she *really* remembered the day she first told me about The Teenage Boy when she was only five and a half years old.

At that time she had handed me a pencil and a little journal book of hers that she used to practice writing. She said, “Majo, write this down because I am only going to tell you one time.”

She said she remembered that day and often sees The Teenage Boy.

Now she handed me a tablet and a pencil and said, “You

better write this down because I am only going to tell you once."

I said, "Yes, that's exactly what you said."

She said, "Majo! I am about to tell you something and you better write it down."

I said, "OH!"

When she tells me that, I have learned to respond immediately, because it is going to be important.

As she started speaking, I wrote rapidly on the paper she had given me.

She said, "One day I was in heaven with Jesus and we went fishing. We had so much fun because we caught so many fish. We took them back to His house. He have a big place like a park out beside His house and it is covered."

I said, "Like a pavilion?"

She said, "Yes, just like a pavilion at a park only really big… HUMONGOUS!"

A BIG GRILL & HUMONGOUS BREAD MACHINE

She continued, "He have a big, big, big grill in there under that pavilion and we cooked the fish on the grill. Jesus cooked a really big loaf of bread. It was huge!"

I asked, "What was the bread like? Was it cornbread? Or maybe was it like regular loaf bread?"

She said, "You know how you make bread in that bread machine and it comes out hot and good and smells so good?"

Incredulous I said, "Jesus used a bread machine?"

Victoria's face lit up as she announced proudly, "Yep, Jesus have a really HUMONGOUS, **GIGANTIC**, ***GINOURMOUS*** bread machine and He make the **biggest** loaf of bread I ever saw.

Lots of people came and we have a big party and we ***never*** ran out of bread. There was always more."

Things are so much bigger and grander in heaven that Victoria has a hard time finding words to describe what she sees. She sometimes has to make up words that are adequate in her mind to match the enormity of heaven.

SINGIN' AND DANCIN'

I said, "Did the eight boys and eight girls come?

Victoria answered, "Yes, but lots and lots of other kids their age came with them."

I asked her, "Was Granny there?"

She quickly answered, "Yes, and all of our relatives came. Some of them came that I didn't even know."

Then I asked, "What about the babies you met when you first went to heaven?"

She replied, "Yep… Alcie and Majolynn and Garbage Baby and Little Victoria came and also a lot of other babies came, too."

I asked, "Was The Teenage Boy there?"

Victoria answered, "Yes… *He* was playing beautiful music and we were dancing… and lots of other teenage kids were there, too. Sport and Rose and lots and lots of teenagers."

Then I asked her about some other people she knew in heaven, "Was Ruth Heflin and Kathryn Kuhlman there?"

She has told us that Ruth Heflin and Kathryn Kuhlman are her teachers in heaven. One time Kathryn wanted to be young that day. She was only sixteen years old and she danced with Victoria all day long.

FAT FREE

She said, “Yep and they danced and danced. It was a big party and we ate the fish and bread. It was the best fish I ever tasted and the bread was so delicious I couldn’t stop eating it.

“But there was always more. In heaven you can eat all you want and you never get fat.”

I said, “Victoria you explained that it was a beautiful park and the pavilion was so very beautiful and the grill was really, really big and the bread machine was humongous… tell me… what did you see when you looked over at the home beside the park.”

JESUS HAS A HOUSE

She got a dreamy smile on her face and said, “It was a beautiful castle.”

That surprised me. I guess I thought that Jesus always sits on a throne, His palms turned up, beckoning to us to come.

I am sure He *is* always beckoning us to come to Him… but we also need to know that heaven is real and real things are happening there all the time.

Things like fish dinners and parties with really hopping music. And the drums are God’s own heartbeat.

Victoria and Jesus danced to the beat of God’s big heart, while The Teenage Boy played beautiful music. Actually, heaven is a real happening place.

JUST SOAK ABOUT IT

After Grandpa took Victoria to go home with Sandi that day, I went and lay down in our prayer room and was listening to one of the soaking CD's by Todd Bentley.

It was about Psalm 84:1-4; 10-11, and Todd was saying… "Your house, Your house, oh Lord, how wonderful are your pavilions, oh Lord. Your altars… My soul yearns for the courts of the Lord"

PAVILLION

> Ps 84:1-4; 10-11
> 1 How lovely is Your tabernacle, O LORD of hosts!
> 2 My soul longs, yes, even faints For the courts of the LORD;
> My heart and my flesh cry out for the living God.
> 3 Even the sparrow has found a home,
> And the swallow a nest for herself,
> Where she may lay her young –

GRILL?

> Even Your altars, O LORD of hosts, My King and my God.
> 4 Blessed are those who dwell in Your house;
> They will still be praising You.
> 10 For a day in Your courts is better than a thousand.
> I would rather be a doorkeeper in the house of my God
> Than dwell in the tents of wickedness.
> 11 For the LORD God is a sun and shield;
> The LORD will give grace and glory;

GOOD FISH

> No good thing will He withhold
> From those who walk uprightly.

Well I could absolutely see what he was talking about; I had just received a first hand description of the Pavilion of the Lord.

The alters… could David have been invited to a wonderful fish dinner in the pavilion of the Lord?

I DO WHAT I SEE MY FATHER DO

> John 5:19-20
> 19 Then Jesus answered and said to them, "Most assuredly, I say to you, the Son can do nothing of Himself, but what He sees the Father do; for whatever He does, the Son also does in like manner.

COOKIN' FISH

> 20 For the Father loves the Son, and shows Him all things that He Himself does; and He will show Him greater works than these, that you may marvel.

When Jesus was on earth, He said I only do what I see my Father do. Could God have been preparing a huge fish dinner the day Jesus had a multitude in front of Him?

He was feeding a lot of people on the Words of Life. They needed food in the natural as well.

Maybe He saw His Father preparing the fish when He looked up to heaven and thanked the Father for the food, Then He broke the small fish and the little loaves on the earth into pieces

HUMONGOUS LOAF OF BREAD

As Jesus was giving the bread and fish to the disciples to feed the people, God sent a bountiful supply of fish and a "humongous" loaf of bread that day to distribute to the hungry people.

Luke 9:12-17
12 When the day began to wear away, the twelve came and said to Him, "Send the multitude away, that they may go into the surrounding towns and country, and lodge and get provisions; for we are in a deserted place here."
13 But He said to them, "You give them something to eat."
And they said, "We have no more than five loaves and two fish, unless we go and buy food for all these people."
14 For there were about five thousand men.
Then He said to His disciples, "Make them sit down in groups of fifty."
15 And they did so, and made them all sit down.

TWELVE BASKETS LEFT OVER

16 Then He took the five loaves and the two fish, and looking up to heaven, He blessed and broke them, and gave them to the disciples to set before the multitude.
17 So they all ate and were filled, and twelve baskets of the leftover fragments were taken up by them.

Could it be that each of the twelve disciples gathered one basket of left over fragments of food?

NOT A NICE MAN

Just before Victoria turned eight years old, she said at the table one day, "I saw Paul."

We said, "Wow! What was he like? Did he say anything?"

She said. "Well, we talked a little. He say that he was very bad down on the earth. He killed a lot of people."

She added, "Paul did not even know how many Christians got killed because of him, until he met them in heaven. He told them he was sorry for that, but they already knew. They really love Paul."

PAUL AND TIMOTHY

One day Victoria and I were propped up on pillows in my bed. I was still recovering after a bad fall that resulted in several fractures in the hip and pelvic area. I was teaching Victoria from Paul's letter to Timothy.

Paul was giving Timothy some important instructions about how he should conduct himself, and give instructions to other leaders. It seemed like an excellent teaching for Victoria.

Paul gave Timothy the following examples.

> 2 Tim 2:1-6
> 2 And the things that you have heard from me among many witnesses, commit these to faithful men who will be able to teach others also.
> 3 You therefore must endure hardship as a good soldier of Jesus Christ.
> 4 No one engaged in warfare entangles himself with the affairs of this life, that he may please him who enlisted him as a soldier.
> 5 And also if anyone competes in athletics, he is not crowned unless he competes according to the rules.
> 6 The hardworking farmer must be first to partake of the crops.

Suddenly I felt a heavenly presence. I looked around. Victoria was staring at the foot of the bed. She said, "Paul is standing there and so is Timothy."

I called Grandpa in so he could enjoy the wonderful presence of the Holy Spirit and this heavenly visit to our home. We felt as though heaven had come to earth.

We just lay there in silent wonder.

Prayer Time

CHAPTER 15

JUST A LITTLE GIRL

VICTORIA'S FAVORITE PRAYERS

There have been some very precious and treasured moments when Victoria would offer her simple but sincere prayers. This is a sampling of some of those moments.

GOODNIGHT & SWEET DREAMS

This sweet little prayer was recorded at the end of one of Sandi's tapes, when she and Victoria were in Brooksville, and we were in Brandon. It was one night when she was six and a half years old as she was preparing for bed that she offered this little gem.

"Goodnight Majo. Grandpa, don't forget about me. You are safe in God's hands. You are His sheep."

PRAYER FOR A FRIEND

Recently one of our good friends called and asked us to pray for her son-in law. A truck hit him as he took the garbage out to the front of his house. He was badly injured

In 2007, Victoria prayed this simple but effective prayer.

> *Dear God,*
> *I don't know who John is but You do.*
> *He's hurt real bad.*
> *Let Jesus touch his body and make him well.*

Fix everything that's broke.
Amen

THANK YOU FATHER

This little prayer is a favorite of Victoria's. We often sing it before our meals in restaurants. Her sweet little voice leads us softly through this song to the tune of Frere Jacques.

Father - Father. Father - Father.
Once again – Once again
Here we are to thank You
Here we are to thank You
Amen – Amen

PROTECT US GOD

This is Victoria's interpretation of an old prayer of Thanks for our food. She has heard on the news about people getting sick and dying from food that they eat in restaurants.

God is Good
God is Great
Let us thank Him for our food
Bow our heads, we all are fed
Thank you God, for our daily bread.
And please don't let it make us fat
And don't let it kill us. Amen

We do have reason to believe that God will prevent the food from poisoning us. Jesus spoke these words just before He ascended into heaven.

Mark 16: 18
And when they drink deadly poison, it will not hurt them. NIV

PRAYERS OF WARFARE

Sometime the prayer time gets very serious. We often have to engage in spiritual warfare. You cannot imagine how it impacts our ability to pray properly, because Victoria *actually sees* what is attacking or harassing us.

SPONSIBILITY

This particular evening when Victoria was six and a half, Sandi, Grandpa and I were finally able to sit down. Dinner was over and everything was cleaned up and put away.

Sandi had worked all day and Grandpa and I had also been busy all day. It was late and we were totally exhausted.

Sandi stretched out on the couch, Grandpa leaned back on the love seat and I was in my massage recliner to relax my tired back.

Victoria was perched on the edge of the couch in front of Mommy. She looked right in front of her face as though someone stood very close to her, face to face.

She said, "Hi! Little angel! What? There's some demons coming? We got's to 'noint the house?"

PLEASE… GIMME A BREAK!

I had raised my head up to listen when she started to talk. Now I let out a sigh and met Sandi's eyes as I let my head go back again in fatigue.

Our eyes agreed, "Let's let this one go by… I'm just too tired to get up and anoint the house."

Then Victoria said, "Majo, this little angel say a word like 'sponsibility."

The three of us heaved a sigh of resignation, as we got to

our feet. Yes. It *was* our responsibility… when we receive a warning… we *must* take action.

We grabbed the large bottle of olive oil and started through the house. We were binding and casting out. We were calling angels to our door.

Victoria totally soaked her little hands and put full handprints of oil on every door, wall and window she could reach… even newly painted walls.

She was saying, “Demons, in the name of Jesus you have to go.”

She did some karate chops and kicks. She also swung her hands and arms as though holding a large sword.

We have repeated this exercise in our home and in Sandi’s home many times.

Sometimes you just gotta fight!

JUST A CUTE LITTLE STORY

In February 2007, we were listening to a talk show and one of the callers became a little ugly.

Victoria said, “They shouldn’t be so angrified. They should just do nice things for each other and be kindful.”

She asked me to turn the radio off. She explained, “They was attitudin’ and I don’t need to hear that.” (had an attitude)

A SPECIAL DAY FOR A SPECIAL GIRL

Cabbage Patch Day

Grandpa, Victoria and I drove away from Brooksville early on this late summer day when Victoria was seven and a half. The heavenly children often travel with us, but this time we only had Little Victoria and The Teenage Boy.

We had called ahead and planned a special day for Victoria. It was a surprise.

We drove straight through to Cleveland, Georgia and stayed overnight.

EXPECTANT MOMMY

The next morning we went to the Babyland General Hospital, birthplace of the wonderful hand sculpted Cabbage Patch babies. This was a great surprise to Victoria. She had Little Victoria and The Teenaged Boy with her and they were excited as we went into the hospital.

We walked through the NICU and saw many little preemie babies in incubators. They were so tiny and precious. Victoria was so carried away with the sweetness of the room and the tiny babies; she could hardly bear to leave. She admitted it reminded her of the little babies in heaven.

Then they announced over the speaker system that mother cabbage was in labor and everyone should come to the delivery area.

LABOR PAINS

We hurried to the delivery room and there we saw a whole patch of cabbages. A nurse was in there working with the mother cabbage that was in labor.

Next they announced that mother cabbage was dilated 9 leaves.

The nurse announced that she was starting an IV of “imagicillon.” As she got that hooked up she went ahead and performed an “easyotomy.” Then the baby came right up through that cabbage.

BOUNCING BABY GIRL

She was a little baby girl with a little blonde curl and blue eyes.

To Victoria's surprise, the nurse called her over and asked if she would like to name this little baby girl.

Victoria was speechless, but grinning. She nodded yes; she would like to name her. She finally whispered that she wanted to name her Maggie.

The nurse wrapped the newborn baby in a blanket and motioned for Victoria to come around to the side. She handed her the baby, so she could bond with her own little Maggie.

Then we went down the hall to the office and let Victoria sign the official adoption papers. She was glowing with happiness as she promised to take good care of Maggie.

This was a little girl's dream come true.

As Grandpa took care of the financial part of it, Victoria and I had to shop for a few necessities in their little shop. We definitely needed a diaper bag and a couple of bottles and some diapers.

Of course, we had to have a car seat. Victoria wanted Maggie to be safe on our journey.

Maggie also needed a change of clothes. We really had fun.

BOOKS FOR BABYLAND

As it turned out, Grandpa discovered that all the nurses and ladies that worked there were sweet Christians.

We all went out to the Suburban. Grandpa got an arm load of books and went back inside. He gave all of them a set of the books. We had copies of 6 Big Angels and Restoring Mommy's Heart with us at that time.

Victoria and I stayed out at the car getting Maggie's car seat strapped in.

Then Grandpa ran back out and said that the ladies wanted Victoria and me to sign their books. Victoria and I were very happy to sign them.

FOREIGN TRAVELER

We left with Maggie and headed to Helen, GA, a small town that looks like it is in Switzerland. As we drove, Victoria was talking softly to Maggie, Little Victoria and The Teenaged Boy.

We walked around visiting the shops. Of course, our favorite was the fudge shop.

We had lunch overlooking the river and then rode the horse drawn carriage.

One of the horses named "Smilin' Bob," smiled at Victoria as we took their picture.

This was a wonderful fun filled day from start to finish, a perfect day for a little girl who has been from the heights of heaven to the pits of the bad place, but still needs a day to be, Just a Little Girl.

CHAPTER 16

ON EARTH AS IT IS IN HEAVEN

We consider ourselves to be ordinary folks who have a deep love and yearning for the things of God. We actively seek His presence and the manifestation of His Glory.

We believe Him when he promised us that His Kingdom would be on the earth as it is in heaven. He has been faithful and we have experienced some very amazing things. If you seek, you too, will find.

We could relate many testimonies of people just like you and me. People who have begun to enjoy the manifestation of the presence of God, are finding Him at home in their private time, in His Secret Place.

> Ps 91:1-2
> He who dwells in the secret place of the Most High
> Shall abide under the shadow of the Almighty.
> 2 I will say of the LORD, "He is my refuge and my fortress;
> My God, in Him I will trust."

In this chapter, I will tell you about a few of our experiences to offer you encouragement to seek and find the manifest presence of the Glory of God.

In February 2006, I had a dream about Israel. When I related the substance of the dream to Sid Roth, he requested that I share it with his TV audience. We were in

Charlotte, NC in June 2006 taping segments for his television broadcast, "It's Supernatural."

He felt there was a significant connection between the dream and the current circumstances in the Middle East. Just a couple of months after we taped the shows, a major conflict erupted between Israel and Lebanon.

GOING TO JERUSALEM

In my dream, Grandpa and I were in Israel with Sandi and Victoria. We were going to Jerusalem. We were standing at a fork in the road. We had our suitcases in our hands and I was carrying my keyboard.

The left road sign said Damascus. The center one said Jerusalem and the one on the right said Jericho.

As we started to take the road to Jerusalem, planes came from the direction of Damascus and started dropping bombs.

We ran into an automobile repair shop. It was a small garage with room for only one car at a time.

I laid my keyboard across the hood of the car that was being repaired. We tried to hide under the narrow work shelf.

Bombs hit and exploded on the garage. The place took a direct hit and shingles, boards and bricks landed on us.

We were hurt and bloody but nothing to compare to the people who had been caught outside. Many people were hurt.

The noise stopped as the planes flew away. I tiptoed to the front of the garage and carefully looked outside to see if it was safe to go out.

As I leaned out and looked up at the sky I saw stuff floating in the air.

The air was thick like gelatin that has not quite set up. A voice spoke out of the thickness...

"THIS IS MY PROTOPLASM. OPEN YOUR MOUTH AND DRINK ME IN... DRINK IN MY DNA! DRINK IN MY ATOMS! DRINK IN MY CELLS! DRINK IN MY RAINBOWS!"

> Ps 81:10
> 10 I am the LORD your God,
> Who brought you out of the land of Egypt;
> Open your mouth wide, and I will fill it.

I realized the stuff floating in the air was just that: DNA, Atoms, Cells and Rainbows. I stepped outside and opened my mouth and started sucking in the thickness of the substance of the Lord. With my hands I was waving the DNA and cells and atoms and rainbows toward my mouth.

As I drank them in, the hurts and injuries disappeared. I was filled with light and airiness and felt as though I could float, I was so filled with lightness. I was also shining from the light of the rainbows that I swallowed.

OPEN YOUR MOUTH AND DRINK!

As I started back into the garage to get my family, I started telling the people on the ground to open their mouth and drink it in. Some of the people did drink and received healing, but others didn't believe me, and kept their injuries.

I walked back inside the garage and told Grandpa, Sandi, and Victoria to come outside. They were hurt and bleeding but they came outside and soon all of us were drinking in the protoplasm of God and being healed. We were laughing and praising the Lord.

Then I went back to check on my keyboard and it was covered with shingles and junk. I placed my hands on the junk at the places where the keys were, and beautiful music came out through the junk.

We shook the dust off our suitcases and my keyboard and headed on down the road to Jerusalem.

DNA OF GOD

Shortly after the filming session with Sid Roth, in June 2006, we were at home in Brandon, Florida.

Grandpa and I went to bed after working late transcribing a tape for the book.

We lay down about midnight. I twisted around for a while trying to get comfortable and finally turned over on my back. I looked up at the ceiling and it was very busy. It looked familiar. I had seen this before.

The DNA was turning, the cells and atoms were spinning and the rainbows were floating around. I glanced around and Grandpa was staring up at the ceiling also.

I asked, “Are you looking up at the ceiling?”

He answered, “Yes.”

I said, “What do you see?”

He replied, “It’s alive!”

I was astonished! I asked him, “Do you see what I see? Do you see the DNA and the atoms and cells and rainbows?”

He said that he saw them, also. We were so surprised that the Lord let us see the same thing.

We didn't know what God wanted us to do. We praised a little... prayed a little... drank Him in ... Then we asked Jesus to cover our home and our family with His Blood and immediately He turned the ceiling Crimson.

We saw the color amber cover a lot of the ceiling. Then the ceiling disappeared and we saw into the vastness of space.

We saw sparks like lightening. We saw stars... then we saw gemstones of different colors.

We saw emeralds, rubies, topaz, and sapphires that seemed to be falling at different times. Not mixed... we would see one color falling and then another. If we closed our eyes, we still saw the stars and gemstones.

We looked at the ceiling for over an hour.

Then, the ceiling was back and seemed to be clear. We got up, made a milkshake, and just talked about the miraculous thing that happened to us. Then we went back to bed.

The ceiling seemed clear as we lay down. Then it was a thick whirling mass of DNA, cells, atoms and rainbows again. We watched the ceiling and just peacefully went to sleep.

The DNA, cells, atoms and rainbows we saw in our ceiling were not shining or supernaturally bright. This experience was of this natural world seen with spiritual vision. We are literally surrounded and upheld by the substance of God in this natural world.

> Hebrews 1: 3
> 3 The Son reflects the Glory of God and shows exactly what God is like. He holds everything together with his powerful word.

The only bright things we saw are naturally bright, such as lightening and the gemstones.

HEAVENLY SUBSTANCE

Victoria has confirmed that the atmosphere in heaven is thicker that the air here on earth. After one of her visits she told us that in the throne room the air is much thicker than other places in heaven.

One time she was near one of the walls of the throne room and saw the thick substance dripping down the wall. She scooped some of it up in her hand and smelled it. It smelled so good she put some of it into her mouth and swallowed it.

When it reached her tummy it started to laugh.

In his book "Home Is Where the Throne Is," Wayne Anderson[12] talks about the substance of heaven. He also says the atmosphere of heaven is thick and has a sweet smell. He could hear music in it.

He says the substance is the pure love of God. It flowed freely between him and God as they expressed love for one another.

I believe that Wayne and Victoria were describing the same substance. Is it possible that this pure love of God is the source of what we call Holy Laughter?

HEAVENLY LIFEGUARD

In 2005 Pat Holloran was visiting our home during the annual IAM Convening. He had not heard about Victoria's fall and trip to heaven. He told us we had fifteen-foot tall warrior angels at all of our doors and there was a large lifeguard angel at the swimming pool slide.

---

[12] Wayne C. Anderson
Standsure Ministries
Meridian, ID 83680
www.standsure.net

The first time I saw the lifeguard angel, he was lying in a position of repose across the top of the pump house that is close to the pool. It was as if he was propped on one elbow with his head resting on his hand. I saw his head, shoulders, and chest and the outline of his hip and thigh and on down his leg.

He was wearing something on his chest that resembled a breastplate that looked brown. It looked like squares tied together with string. Almost like a tank top.

I had the impression that he had on a white garment that wasn't very long. I saw part of his knee and shin.

As Victoria and Stephanie got into the pool together to swim, he lifted up about six feet above the roof of the pump house and remained in the same reclining position.

He just swung out and drifted over the pool to a place in the air just above Victoria and Stephanie as if to be close to them if they needed him.

We had never seen the angels until Pat told us about them. After we were aware of their presence, we began to ask God to let us be able to see them. While we do not see as clearly as Victoria, we can see the angel at the pool and often see more up on top of the pump house.

The lifeguard angel stays at the ladder of the slide most of the time. He is about twelve feet tall. We see him in the form of a misty shape. You can see the trees behind him as you look at him but it is like looking through antique glass or at the heat waves that come up from a hot road.

Many people who come to our house can see him.

HEAVENLY VISITATION

One day Victoria and I were busy in the classroom, when Sandi called and said she had finished work early and we needed to bring Victoria to her right away.

We quickly got her ready to go and she left with Grandpa while I stayed home. In fact, I was still in the classroom and I told the kids from heaven who were attending school that day that they were welcome to stay but Victoria had to leave. I told them I was sorry she forgot to say goodbye.

I did not think any more about it at the time. I just went about my normal routine. You have to understand that I do not see the children clearly, as Victoria does, but I know they are with us.

That night as Grandpa and I were preparing for sleep we were just laying there praying and ending the day. The lights were off and the room was dark. We were not asleep yet.

As I was just silently looking up I began to see a lot of movement at our ceiling level. I asked Grandpa if he saw anything up there and he told me that he did. At first we could not distinguish what we were seeing but later the images became clearer. They came closer... some of the moving forms we saw were so tiny we could not make out what they were. Then they started to come *very* close to our faces.

As they began to take shape, we could tell we were seeing tiny little babies. Mostly we only saw flashes of feet, legs, hands or heads. They were moving fast as if they were cavorting all over the place. It appeared that they were turning cartwheels, jumping, tumbling and running.

We watched for a long time and enjoyed the company of the heavenly children. The only thing I could think of to do was tell them they are welcome and that we love them.

SUPPER WITH JESUS

Grandpa and I frequently take communion at home.

Several times a day is not too often.

One night we were preparing to go to sleep and were taking communion at The Table of the Lord. We were propped up against our pillows on the bed. We do this often at different times of the day or night.

We are never in a hurry when we have a meal with Jesus. As we were praying and enjoying the fellowship, I closed my eyes. When I did, I saw Jesus sitting at the table across from us. When I told Grandpa what I was seeing he told me he was seeing the same thing.

THE TABLE OF THE LORD

Wayne Anderson's book titled "The Table of the Lord" is an in-depth study that teaches the benefits of partaking of communion often. We highly recommend you get the book and study it and confirm what you read with the scriptures.

Great healing in body, soul and spirit happens during communion.

Wayne has studied and practiced the act of communion for many years.

We must not let the longstanding traditions of man dictate how and when we visit His table.

Communion is not just a religious ritual. The Table of the Lord is an intimate time of fellowship with Jesus. It is all about the shed blood and the power that it represents.

TWINKIES AND RC COLA

God releases His power to us during our time of intimacy with Him.

In his book, Wayne said we could use anything for the bread and wine. He cautioned us to not get too religious about it. He has used animal crackers and 7up and he sometimes has a good time at the Lord's Table with a Twinkie and an RC Cola as he drives from one place to another.

He teaches us to say Christ's body was freely given for our sins, not broken.

Isaiah prophesied that no bones would be broken and the Gospels bear that out. They pierced Him but none of His bones were broken.

It is a religious tradition to say "Lord, this is your body", as we... **snap!** ... break the wafer or bread, "that was broken for us."

When we break the symbolic body of Christ, we are speaking a prophecy that is detrimental to the body of Christ.

This prophetic word may be part of the reason the Body of Christ... the Church... is broken apart into so many fragments.

Enjoy a relaxed intimate dinner with the Lord Jesus Christ. Do not fear or hesitate to come to the Table of the Lord often.

BAXLEY, GEORGIA

In January 2007, the pastor of El Shaddai Revival Worship Center in Baxley, Georgia, Ila Mae Mc Leighton, invited us for three days of services. She had seen us on Sid Roth and wanted to meet Victoria, and let her people hear about heaven first hand.

On Friday night, we told the precious story again of God's mercy and grace when He rescued Victoria and let her come back to us.

It was the first time we came up against a spirit of unbelief.

I thought it was only with one person, but it made the service a little tough. It was hard to get into the anointing of the Holy Spirit.

However, after we spoke, as we ministered to the one or two, who came forward, some people left. Apparently the unbelief walked out at that time, because more people came on up to let us pray for them to see into the supernatural. We had a wonderful time of ministry.

When we got back to the hotel we prayed that God would lift the spirit of unbelief and bless this town and these people.

We now believe that everything that happened in Baxley was exactly God's will. We didn't know it at that time but the room was full of intercessors and people who were to become our staunchest supporters.

We were in a safe place when we had to battle the spirit of unbelief. We had to learn to minister, while under attack. We call Baxley, SCHOOL OF MINISTRY 101.

GOD'S RV

When Sandi prayed on Saturday night, it was a *very anointed* and forceful exhortation. We felt the heavens open and glory filled the room.

That made it easy to tell about Victoria seeing God's portable throne or "Heavenly RV" at the baby place and to tell about the glory that happened as both of us saw it at Nashville, Tennessee. We used the scripture in Ezekiel to describe God's RV.

After church, Victoria said, "When Mommy prayed... the heavens opened and a lot of stuff came pouring in." She could not tell us about it at that time.

We have to wait until God tells her it is all right for us to know.

Later she said that the Living creatures came in and God's throne was there.

HEAVENLY HAY RIDE IN BAXLEY GEORGIA

That night in our hotel room after the wonderful service, we were preparing the message for the Sunday morning service. The Lord had been dealing with me about what I should tell the people.

He had instructed me to tell about the "great cloud of witnesses." I was reluctant to approach what could be a controversial and misunderstood message.

As I lay in bed praying and trying to prepare, I began to see a vision of an old-fashioned farm wagon. The wagon appeared to be very old and was unpainted. It had iron rimmed wooden wheels and was quite large.

As the vision became clearer, I could see that the wagon was full of babies and children. I could make out the details of their appearance. I could see the color of their hair and eyes.

One little boy had black hair and freckles and brown eyes. I could even make out that he was waving at me. All of them were grinning at me.

I softly said, "Sandi are you awake? She said she was. I told her what I was seeing and asked if she could see them… she answered and said she could see the wagon but the kids were not clear to her.

I knew that God had sent them to me and He wanted me to tell about them. I lay there laughing with the children in the hay wagon and praising God for over an hour.

VICTORIA'S CLASSMATES

The next morning I told about the little babies that come to our classroom. I told about praying with them for the healing of children who are very ill. We have many pictures on our bulletin board. Some of these children are pulling ahead and getting better.

I mentioned Katy's little girl who always comes and brings Jesus to her mommy's rescue. I let them know that Granny, my mother often comes to see Victoria and Grandpa's mother has been at the dinner table with us.

I was preaching to the choir, because Ila Mae's Grandson had been telling her that he saw his grandfather... and she believed him. She has believed for years that we, as Christians ought to be able to travel to heaven and back in the spirit.

HANDSOME PREACHER MAN

Weeks later, Victoria told us that she saw a preacher man come and stand by Sister Ila Mae Mc Leighton on that Saturday night when Mommy prayed and stuff poured in. This saint had gone on to heaven the year before. He was the Pastor of this congregation, and Ila Mae's husband.

When we called to tell Ila Mae some weeks later, she was delighted because it confirmed that her grandson was actually seeing into the spirit and not just missing his grandfather.

He had already told his mommy that he saw his grandfather standing beside his grandmother's chair on that Saturday night at the same time Victoria saw him.

That precious little boy is now seeing into the spirit. He and his little sister often see angels and went to heaven together a few nights ago.

God is calling many children at a very young age. They are speaking up about the knowledge of the Glory of God.

DIGGIN' UP SEEDS

We recently went back to Baxley and as I was praying on Sunday morning before church, the Holy Spirit revealed to me a word that I had to speak to these people at this time.

It seems I always get to walk through the tough lessons at Baxley, surrounded by loving intercessors, friends and this lovely lady pastor. God is very Gracious.

The word was this; if we have the seeds of racism and bigotry in our hearts... it opens a gate and the forces of evil have legal authority to come in and steal and destroy our families.

We, the body of Christ, must be very sure that we are not contaminated in this way against any person, race or ethnic group.

DANGEROUS RAILIN'

Another surprising word that I had to say, right in the middle of these wonderful meetings about a little girl's trips to heaven was, don't rail against Satan.

I warned the intercessors to leave that to God. They have authority in the earth, but the rest is God's war.

Several women came and talked to me after church and said our message was talking to them.

One told me that she railed against Satan last year and within a month she had cancer. They all had stories to tell me about illness in their body and they had not even known the reason why.

Zech 3:1-2
3:1 Then he showed me Joshua the high priest standing before the angel of the LORD, and Satan standing at his right side to accuse him.
2 The LORD said to Satan, "The LORD rebuke you, Satan! The LORD, who has chosen Jerusalem, rebuke you!
NIV

2 Peter 2:10, 11, 12
Bold and arrogant, these men are not afraid to slander celestial beings;
11 yet even angels, although they are stronger and more powerful, do not bring slanderous accusations against such beings in the presence of the Lord.
12 but these men blaspheme in matters they do not understand.

Hosea 4:6
6 My people are destroyed from lack of knowledge.

I am not advising you to walk in fear. I am asking you to arm yourselves with knowledge. There are some good books about the battle belonging to the Lord. Read them... gain the knowledge of the power and the authority of the Lord.

SMART IN HEAVEN

Victoria told us just recently that she feels like she is twenty years old in heaven. She knows a lot up there and is a lot smarter. More than when she is here. She teaches a class of kids in heaven who are thirteen and fourteen years old and "Little Victoria" who is almost four years old already teaches a class of the tiny aborted babies.

Victoria teaches a class of twelve kids. That day, as she told me about it, she taught math and language.

She said the kids really love to do show and tell. They brought small live animals to show and tell about. One child brought a small little rabbit that looked almost like Victoria's pet rabbit, Cookie.

The day that we were talking about the classroom in heaven, she said that she had gone really early in the morning to teach.

CHAPTER 17

FRENCH CONNECTION

WEAVING A TAPESTRY

If you read our first book, you will recognize some of the people and events in this chapter. God has connected us to people and arranged encounters that still astound us. Over time, the connections have been woven into a beautiful tapestry designed by God. We stand in awe of Him.

This is an example of one part of the tapestry God is weaving with our lives.

WHY US LORD?

Have you ever wondered what God is doing in your life?

We had no idea what God was really doing on September 2, 2003 when Victoria fell nine feet from our swimming pool slide to the concrete deck below and was unharmed.

We thought God had just provided an awesome miracle by saving Victoria from serious injury or even death. That illusion lasted about three hours.

We still do not know exactly what God is doing in our life. Our understanding of it changes daily.

What we do know is that He is weaving a tapestry that is beautiful. The threads are His people doing His will. Many people are still faceless and only time will reveal them.

THREAD ONE

By the end of September 2003 we knew about the aborted babies Victoria met at the Baby Place.

Early in October we talked to David Alsobrook and sent him our notes. We talked on the phone many times and he decided that he should tell about the heavenly visit in his monthly newsletter.

In February 2004 we met him in Ashland, Virginia for camp meeting. Before he spoke that night, he had us come up to the platform and tell about Victoria and the aborted babies in heaven.

He told the people he had done an insert for his April 2004 newsletter. Many people signed up to be put on his mailing list.

A lady named Elizabeth Szeremeta, who lives in Quebec, received David's newsletter because she had been on his mailing list for years.

She read it and kept it with her Bible. She believed every word. She had no idea what God had planned for her.

THREAD TWO

We had assembled a few episodes of "heavenly happenings" and had the beginnings of a manuscript. We let Victoria pick out the color for the cover. It was hot pink and had a little picture of her on the front.

We copied the manuscript and David's newsletter and had them ready to share with Revivalist Joshua Mills in August 2004. He was at The ROC, in Dover, Florida and Victoria really liked him.

She wanted him to know that she went to heaven. She seldom shares her experience, but Joshua was special.

He came back in November for another series of meetings at the ROC.

He had read the manuscript and asked us to speak at his winter camp meeting in Orlando, Florida in January 2005.

WRITE THE BOOK

God had told us to write a book about Victoria's experiences in heaven. But by early January, 2005 even though we had added a few more episodes to the manuscript, we were far from having a book ready.

In fact, not only did we not have a book finished, we didn't know what to do at all. We thought we needed a publisher to polish it up and turn it into a book. We thought there was just no way *we* could write a book by ourselves.

We were simply going to go to the camp meeting and tell about Victoria and the glory of heaven. We felt that most of all we wanted people to know about the aborted babies and the love they have for their mothers.

We thought we were going to speak that one time and that would be the end of it until a publisher "fixed" our book. But God...

A DREAM FROM GOD

Seven days before the camp meeting date, Kim Clement came to me in a dream.

I did not know Kim and had never heard him speak. In fact, I had never seen a picture of him. I had only heard his name.

In the dream, he held up the manuscript that we had given Joshua Mills in August.

He said, "I have read this. If it were me I would make as many copies of this as you can and take it to Joshua's camp meeting."

I asked, "In a binder like that?"

He answered, "Yes, in a binder just like this. This could be the spark that ignites a great revival in Central Florida."

When I woke up I related the dream to Grandpa and told him what Kim said. He asked me to describe him and then went on the Internet and found his website.

It was the same man that was in my dream.

So Grandpa and I prayed all that day. The next day we started to work on the book.

After three days, we had it cobbled together in some kind of order. We were not sure of the sequence of events because Victoria was very private about her experiences.

Often she would not answer our questions.

It was rough and small, only 78 pages, but it was what we had. We printed them at a copy shop and put them together at home with an ancient binding machine that uses plastic combs.

We did 100 manuscripts with pink covers.

Even then, Holy Spirit anointed it and as we read it to proof it, Grandpa and I would cry. As we read about the aborted babies and the garbage baby, we often could hardly see the print.

FIRST CAMP MEETING

We showed up at Joshua's winter Camp meeting, January 2005 held in Orlando. They made room for us on one of the book tables. We had 100 homemade manuscripts with Victoria's little picture on the front.

We also had a box of the four-page insert that had been in David Alsobrook's Newsletter. This gracious man of God had shipped them to us totally free.

We put out a few of our manuscripts for sale and a stack of the brochures with a sign that said, "FREE." We were a little embarrassed because the tables were full of beautiful books and CD's.

When it was our turn to speak, Grandpa delivered a brief introduction and turned the mike over to me. As I was speaking, he saw a vision. In the vision, he saw a fireworks rocket go up high into the sky from the center of the audience.

At its highest point it exploded and created many sparks that landed in different places all over the world. Everywhere a spark landed another rocket went off and exploded and on and on.

THREAD THREE

A lady who lives in Ft. Myers, Florida bought a book. Her name is Pat Spigner and she was the former praise and worship leader at Abundant Love Christian Fellowship in Washington, DC. Tom and Sue Bruener pastor this inner-city church.

Pat read the book and sent it to a friend who attends Abundant Love Christian Fellowship.

THREAD FOUR

Sue Bruener got her hands on it and knew instantly that she needed more copies for the hurting women in Washington, DC. I received her e-mail at the same time Grandpa was on a plane headed to DC to do a consulting job. It was a God thing. I boxed up 25 books and sent them overnight to his hotel room. When he landed, I told him to call Sue, a pastor in DC, who wanted some books.

He called... they picked him up the next evening and from there the book has gone around the world. They kept ordering more and mailing out more. Every batch we printed would have a little more information in it, as Victoria revealed more and more of the wonders of heaven.

THREAD FIVE

Sue sent one to her friend, a lady named Carole in France. Carole received it just before attending a Christian Conference in Paris. She was reading as fast as she could. She was trying to drink it in before the service started.

Holy Spirit said, "GIVE THE BOOK TO THE PEOPLE IN FRONT OF YOU."

The people she gave it to sent me an e-mail three days later. They said they were at a conference in Paris, and received the manuscript from a woman they did not know.

They were publishers and asked for permission to translate the book into French. They felt that God had handed them the book. Their names are Ann and Malgwyn Elmer.[13] Ann wrote the book titled "Transported by the Lion of Judah."

A few days after we heard from the Elmers, I contacted Carole to let her know what had happened as a result of her obedience.

---

[13] Editions de la Source
Chemin des Ecarts
78640 Neauphle le Ecarts, France
www.editionsdelasource.fr

I told her I had written the book about Victoria's trip to heaven and how much our life had changed as a result. I thanked her for obeying the voice of the Holy Spirit.

I told her the people she gave the book to were publishers in France.

When she responded she told me that just a few weeks before she attended the conference she had prayed that the Lord would use her to get Christian books published in French.

She said she did not know why she was surprised that God answered her prayer so fast.

She felt like the French people would be blessed by Victoria's story. She is praying that her two young daughters will also be used in revival in France.

One of her daughters has visions where she sees Jesus, angels and heaven. Victoria's story and her daughter's experiences are similar.

She told us the Lord had said through prophetic words that He is going to use children in the French revival and that surely our books would have an impact.

THREAD SIX

In October 2006 I received an e-mail from Elizabeth in Quebec. The subject line simply said "Blue Glass." I am always curious so I opened it.

Elizabeth said she really enjoyed Victoria's book and was wondering if the blue glass under God's throne is really blue sapphire.

She said there was a scripture in Exodus that refers to "Sapphire stone under his feet." Also, the foundations of the walls of the new Jerusalem include blue sapphire stones.

Ex 24:10
10 and they saw the God of Israel. And there was under His feet as it were a paved work of sapphire stone, and it was like the very heavens in its clarity.
Rev 21:19
19 The foundations of the wall of the city were adorned with all kinds of precious stones: the first foundation was jasper, the second sapphire, the third chalcedony, the fourth emerald,

It was a short note and I had no clue what was to come. I thought she was referring to the blue under God's Throne that Victoria drew that was on the back cover of the book.

However the scripture just above the one she quoted in Exodus 24, helped me in a very real and unusual way. Some believe that no one can see God and live.

This scripture so clearly shows that God can be and do anything He wants. He can kill you or not, at His desire. Moses and Aaron along with some priests and seventy elders went up to the mountain and saw God. They ate with Him and He did not kill them.

MOSES AND AARON AND SEVENTY TWO MORE

Ex 24:9-11
9 Then Moses went up, also Aaron, Nadab, and Abihu, and seventy of the elders of Israel,

SAW GOD OF ISRAEL AND SAPPHIRE STONE

10 and they saw the God of Israel. And there was under His feet as it were a paved work of sapphire stone, and it was like the very heavens in its clarity.

GOD DID NOT RAISE HIS HAND AGAINST THEM

11 But on the nobles of the children of Israel He did not lay His hand. So they saw God, and they ate and drank.

SHINY FACE

Victoria said she could not see all of God's face because it was too shiny, but He let her see His eyes, His hair, His hands, knees and feet. She also saw His robe and the gloriousness of His rainbow.

When Elizabeth wrote to me about the blue glass, she opened up these scriptures that I had forgotten and the Lord gave me revelation about them.

However, God had a very different and important reason for having Elizabeth get in touch with me.

I received another e-mail from Elizabeth that just wiped me out. I believe you will also be affected deeply by the message God gave to this humble servant.

THE FRENCH CONNECTION

Because I promptly answered a short question from Elizabeth, she responded in a very unusual manner. She wrote to me in great detail about a vision she had in 2005.

This is the substance of that e-mail

> *Dear Mrs. Pennington, Thank you for taking time to reply.*
>
> *Last year, I had a vision of Jesus. He was holding a two cell fetus. The fetus spoke to me and relayed a message from heaven.*
>
> *The fetus said that a whole company of very young unborn children got together and wrote a song (in French) to their mothers on earth.*
>
> *I speak simple French, but last year, my French was not quite good enough to write a song like that. The melody is beautiful.*

Jesus told me that it was destined for the French-speaking people. I did translate it into English and Polish. It works in the other two languages also, but really, it was meant to be done in French.

The Lord said He would allow me to do an English translation only because in Quebec some singers might want to perform a bilingual version.

Anyhow, the song has traveled all over the world.

A week after the vision the Lord explained to me that different events in my life prepared me to receive this vision.

One of these events was an account I read in David Alsobrook's newsletter about Victoria's experience.

Of course, there were other events as well. I am very good at taking down music, so the fetus sang the song to me until I got it all down.

I saw the same child later in another vision. It was a little older.

Then about two weeks ago, the Lord told me to look up Victoria's website.

As soon as I saw the book, I knew I had to have it.

Thank you so much for publishing it. Elizabeth

ELIZABETH AND STEPHANIE

I asked our daughter Stephanie to send a copy of her poem book, "Restoring Mommy's Heart", to Elizabeth. We were traveling at the time and could not respond.

Elizabeth responded with another surprising coincidence. She told Stephanie that before she read the book, as she opened it, one phrase jumped out and hit her like a thunderbolt: That phrase was, “God gave me to you.”

When she wrote the text of the English version of the song, she wrote exactly the same phrase in one line of the song: “God gave me to you.” That was before she had even seen Stephanie’s book of poems.

THE YOUNGEST OF ALL

This is the transcription of Elizabeth’s encounter with Jesus and the aborted baby. This two-cell fetus was probably the result of the morning after pill, which has been in use in France for decades. It has recently been approved for use in the US.

ELIZABETH’S VISION

My name is Elizabeth Szeremeta, and on August 16, 2005 a little after 10 pm I was at home at Rawdon, Quebec, Canada.

Suddenly I noticed that the light in the dining room where I was seated at the table began to get brighter and brighter.

In my spirit, I knew that soon heaven would come down to earth.

I waited… Jesus came…

I have read the accounts of Sister Faustina, a Polish nun who saw and described Jesus.

The wonderful Jesus that I saw fit her description, except he was more golden, more glorious. His hair had brilliant highlights. Surrounding Him were minuscule particles of gold dust, which danced in the air around him.

Jesus began to speak. He said he was holding an aborted embryo in his hand. He let me see a close-up of this embryo, as if I were looking through a magnifying glass, so that I could scrutinize all the details:

I had a moment of uneasiness. This embryo had neither arms nor legs. There were no details, which resembled a baby.

All I could see was two cells fused together. Each cell had a darker spot. I was made to understand that this spot was the door through which one could enter in… in order to obtain all the details on the future development of the baby.

Here is an excerpt of our conversation:

Jesus said, "This aborted baby has a message for you."

I said, "Jesus, why are you speaking to me in French? You know I understand English or Polish better."

Jesus said, "This message is destined for French-speaking people."

Suddenly, I realized I had a perfect mastery of the French language. I was thrilled.

The Baby embryo said to me, "I am a baby who is now living in heaven, along with thousands upon thousands of other babies who are growing up with me. Together we wrote a letter to our mothers, who are still living on Earth."

WHY ME LORD?

I asked, "Why did you choose me to deliver this message? I have never experienced an abortion."

Jesus answered, "Because you are able to write music."

Baby embryo answered also, "We like you because you know rejection, as we knew it, while we were on Earth." Then I started to take down the song, as the baby dictated it to me by singing it, phrase by phrase, note by note.

I noticed that I could take all the time in the world, for the job to be well done. No one was in a hurry. Whenever I was finished, I asked some more questions.

I asked, "Jesus, why did you choose this embryo, in particular, to deliver this message?"

Jesus answered, "Because it was the youngest."

I was made to understand that right from the moment of conception, one is already a person.

I asked, "Is this embryo a girl or a boy?"

Jesus said, "I won't answer that question. This embryo represents all of the aborted girls and boys who are now growing up in heaven"

A SPECIAL GRACE

I asked, "Does the baby have a name? If not, may I give it a name?"

Jesus answered, "No, a special grace will accompany this song each time it will be sung.

"I will let all mothers of aborted babies, who listen to this song know how many girls, how many boys they have rejected.

"If they will repent and decide to consecrate their lives to me, I will give these mothers an opportunity to choose themselves, the names for their aborted children."

I said, "So this baby is waiting for its real mother to pick a name for him?"

Jesus answered, ***"You have understood correctly. This song will be sung here and there, all over the world."***

MY DEAREST MOMMY

By

Elizabeth Szeremeta

ENGLISH VERSION

My Dearest Mommy

My dearest Mommy, I am your own child.
God gave me to you, but then you aborted me.
I see you crying, your heart out for me,
And I'm telling you, that I love you,
Oh Mom, I love you.

My Dearest Mommy, as I watch you from Heaven,
I want to say, that I love you so much,
And at the end of your life's journey,
I want you to come and live
in Heaven with me.

My Dearest Mommy, up in my Heavenly home,
The strong arms of Jesus
hold me with such great love.
I see the splendor and
Joy of all the saints
We're all so glad
that we can
live here forever.

My Dearest Mommy
Jesus does understand
He wants to forgive and to
Give you His peace and His Joy.
Open your heart,
Give your whole life to Him
And when you do, you'll see,
You will be happy.

Chapter 18

VICTORIA'S 8th BIRTHDAY

Victoria and Sandi were having dinner with Grandpa and me around the breakfast bar in the kitchen.

Victoria started telling us about her birthday party in heaven.

HAPPY BIRTHDAY VICTORIA!

On Victoria's eighth birthday, they had a big party at the Baby and Children's Place.

It was wonderful. Everybody came to celebrate. Teenage boy was playing really hoppin' music and they were having so much fun.

Jesus was funnier than goofers. He dressed funny and His hair was pinkish bluish. He was still a clown but he was differenter than he was at "Little Victoria's" birthday party.

He looked so funnier!

PARTY POOPERS

Then the devil and his demons started singing really loud screechy songs to try to ruin her party. She said, "We could hear them."

I asked, "Did you have a good party anyway?"

She said, "It was better than good... cause we had louder music than him.

"We had piñatas and all gifts and candy and ICE CREAM and everything. We were swimming and diving and having so much fun."

Victoria had just jumped from really high up, down into the River of Life at a really deep part that formed a huge pool. She said it felt like she was flying.

She saw Satan watching her with anger on his face, as he flew over her.

She said, "I looked up and he looked at me with a mad face."

> Job 1: 6 One day the angels came to present themselves before the Lord, and Satan also came with them. The Lord said to Satan, "Where have you come from?"

Victoria told me that Satan went before God and God asked him that same question. She heard God say to Satan, "Where have you come from?"

Satan said, "Victoria's eighth Birthday Party."

Then Satan approached God. He said, "I am getting sick and tired of all this childish nonsense."

God answered, **"THIS IS NO CHILDISH NONSENSE! THIS IS MY WILL!"**

I WAS CHOSEN

Just after Victoria turned eight years old she made a proclamation that startled her mother out of a deep sleep.

They had just had their bible stories and prayer and Sandi had gratefully drifted down into peaceful sleep.

Suddenly Victoria sat straight up in bed, and in her deep voice of authority announced, "I was chosen to be the leader of the prophet of Isaiah."

Sandi looked around for a pencil and paper or the tape recorder and nothing was available.

She glanced at the clock and realized that since I am a night hawk, she would probably be safe to call me.

When she told me what Victoria had just said, I wrote it down and then asked, "Is that all she said? She didn't say what this means?"

Sandi said no, that was it, hung up the phone and went back to sleep.

I started reading in Isaiah, looking for anything about the leaders of the prophets. Of course, Isaiah has sixty-six chapters. Soon, I was falling asleep, too.

We began asking different preachers and prophets and nobody had a clue. I kept reading in the Old Testament prophets looking for a reference to "the leader of the prophets."

At that time, the Lord also had us looking for all mention of the KNOWLEDGE OF THE GLORY OF THE LORD that was in the bible. We knew prophesy was being fulfilled every day and God's Glory was in the earth in an awesome way.

One reference to the knowledge of the Lord was in Isaiah 11: 9. As I read the eleventh chapter of Isaiah, I found what Victoria meant. I believe she is one of the children chosen to be a type and a forerunner of the end time, for signs and wonders, as mentioned in this chapter.

I believe one of her teachers in heaven had been teaching her chapter 11 of Isaiah and that she is one of the "little" children chosen to lead and to share "the knowledge of the Glory of the Lord" that she has seen in heaven and in the earth.

> Isaiah 11: 6
> Then wolves will live in peace with lambs, and leopards will lie down to rest with goats.
>
> Calves, lions and young bulls will eat together,
> And a little child shall lead them.

STILL NOT THE END

Other Books Offered By
Big Angels Press

RESTORING MOMMY'S HEART

By
Stephanie Petrus

This series of poems was written as a companion to
6 BIG... BIG... BIG... ANGELS
This heart-gripping book relates the stories of the babies in heaven from the time before they were given up by their mommies until they are grown up. Follow them from when the "choice" was made, to the day they would have been born, to their first birthday and when they are grown.
Listen to the heart wrenching cries of the mommy as she realized what she had done. Watch the healing as she cried out to Jesus for forgiveness and found that in Him her dreams would be restored and her recompense would be seven times seven.

$7.00 USD plus S/H
Big Angels Press
Valrico, Florida
813-681-4993
www.6bigangels.com

The Original Book Of
Victoria's Heavenly Experiences

6 BIG... BIG... BIG... ANGELS

By
Mary Jo Pennington

If you have not read the first book about Victoria and her extraordinary introduction into God's Supernatural Realm, this is a must read.

What could have been a fatal accident, God used to launch Victoria into the destiny He has for her. You do not want to miss a single episode of her amazing experiences into the Glory of the Lord.

$15.00 USD plus S/H
Big Angels Press
Valrico, Florida
813-681-4993
www.6bigangels.com

Coming Soon!!

The First In A Series Of Children's Books

Mary Jo is writing a series of children's books based on Victoria's experiences in heaven as related in

6 BIG... BIG... BIG... ANGELS

These will be written as if Victoria is telling the story herself.

The title of the first book will be

I HEARD GOD YELL:
SAVE THE CHILDREN!
CATCH VICTORIA!

Illustrations will be provided by our granddaughter

Tara Pennington

Watch our web site for available date

Big Angels Press
Valrico, Florida
813-681-4993
www.6bigangels.com

Sid Roth's
Messianic Vision

5/22 – 26/06
Mary Jo Pennington
+ Don

Media Player

T9 Sid Roth
1-800-548-1918
(for Mary Jo newsletter)